ETERNAL PASSION
IN ENGLISH POETRY

ETERNAL PASSION
IN ENGLISH POETRY

Selected by

EDITH WHARTON and ROBERT NORTON

with the collaboration of

GAILLARD LAPSLEY

Granger Index Reprint Series

BOOKS FOR LIBRARIES PRESS
FREEPORT, NEW YORK

STANDARD BOOK NUMBER:
8369-6047-5

LIBRARY OF CONGRESS CATALOG CARD NUMBER:
77-76950

MANUFACTURED
BY
HALLMARK LITHOGRAPHERS, INC.
IN THE U.S.A.

PREFACE

EVERY anthology is always some one person's anthology —yours or mine or his; and the fact that no two can ever be alike ought to be a sufficient excuse for adding another to those already existing.

But in the present case the compilers feel that they need not even excuse themselves for not excusing themselves. As far as they know, their attempt is one of the first to gather between two covers a selection of the most beautiful (or what they believe to be the most beautiful) of English love-poems, lyrical and other. Is it because almost all preceding anthologists have taken it for granted that, in the long line of selections of English poetry, there surely must be many devoted to this supreme category—that when sea and forest, open road and city street, the temple and the tavern, have all furnished their chosen specimens of inspiration, the mightiest of motive-powers could hardly have been forgotten? Or is it because an over-abundance of material was assumed, and the choice avoided as too arduous? At any rate, the field seems still relatively free, and the compilers feel themselves in a position to ask that the following selection of poems shall be given, till further notice, the unqualified title they have chosen for it.

The ruling motive of their selection has, of course, been that of personal preference. They offer to lovers of English verse what they believe to be a choice comprehending the most beautiful passages of love-poetry in the language. No antiquarian limitations, no pedantic search for the unfamiliar, no sense of the obligation to include such or such a poem because it has had the honours of previous selection, or to exclude another because it has been too often thus honoured, has been allowed to hamper their free choice. These are poems read aloud again and again by the winter fireside, and again and again found enchanting and satisfying to reader and listeners.

It may be of interest to add one word to this preliminary. The anthologists found with wonder, as they proceeded in their choice, that the rank taken by the love-poems in the total production of each poet is almost always in inverse ratio to the greatness of the poet. It may be open to discussion whether the rule applies to Shakespeare, because the Sonnets can be weighed only against fragments torn from the text of some mighty whole; one cannot, for instance, put any one sonnet in one scale, and the whole of *Romeo and Juliet* in the other, and say, "Choose!"

But in every other instance it seems to result from a careful winnowing of the field that in the work of the supremely great English poets the love-poem is not supreme. This is so obviously apparent in the case of Milton, Keats, Shelley, Coleridge, and Wordsworth (though he wrote one of the most perfect of English love-poems) that the point does not need pressing, and it is more curious to call attention to the constancy with which the reverse holds true, and the minor poets reach their highest height in the love-poem.

Just between the greatest and the less, astride on the two

peaks, Robert Browning, in this category, proclaims himself, if not supreme, yet most abundant. His most beautiful poetry is certainly his love-poetry, and that he wrote more of it worth preserving than any one other English poet, will be found, on consulting the table of contents, to be the opinion of this particular group of anthologists.

The problem of the relative importance of love-poetry in the whole work of a poet is too complex to be dealt with here; but perhaps a hint toward its solution may be found in the fact that the only emotion to which "all thoughts, all passions, all delights" minister in the average man is but one among many in the breasts of those who, Admirals on the high seas of poetry, thrill to all the "tremors sent below by breezes striking the higher sails."

EDITH WHARTON

ACKNOWLEDGMENTS

For their courteous permission to reprint certain poems in this volume, thanks are due to:

The Macmillan Company, New York, Macmillan & Co., Ltd., London, and the Representatives of the Author, for "On a Lost Opportunity" and "St. Valentine's Day," from *The Poetical Works of Wilfrid Scawen Blunt;*

The Clarendon Press, Oxford, for "Awake My Heart," "So Sweet Love Seemed," and "When Death to Either Shall Come," from *The Shorter Poems of Robert Bridges;*

The Macmillan Company, New York, Macmillan & Co., Ltd., London, and the Executors of the Author, for "Jessie," from *Collected Poems,* by T. E. Brown;

Mrs. Henry Cust for "Non Nobis," from *Occasional Poems* by Henry Cust;

The Macmillan Company, New York, Macmillan & Co., Ltd., London, and the Representatives of the Author for "The Going," from *Collected Poems* by Thomas Hardy;

Macmillan & Co., Ltd., London, and the Executors of the Author, for "What Is to Come," from *Poems* by William Ernest Henley;

Mrs. Rudyard Kipling, Macmillan & Co., Ltd., London, The Macmillan Company of Canada, Ltd., Toronto, and to Doubleday, Doran & Co., Inc., New York, for "The Love Song of Har Dyal," from *Plain Tales from the Hills* (copyright, 1899, 1927), by Rudyard Kipling;

Charles Scribner's Sons, New York, and to Constable and Company Limited, London, for two sonnets from "Modern Love" and three stanzas from "Love in the Valley" from *Poetical Works,* by George Meredith;

ACKNOWLEDGMENTS

Burns Oates & Washbourne, Ltd., London, and to Mr. Wilfrid Meynell, owner of copyright, for "Renouncement," by Alice Meynell;

G. Bell & Sons, Ltd., London, for "A Farewell," by Coventry Patmore;

Macmillan & Co., Ltd., London, and the Representatives of the Author, for "A Bride Song," from *The Poetical Works of Christina Rossetti;*

William Heinemann, Ltd., London, for "The Oblation," "Erotion," and "The Triumph of Time," from *Collected Poetical Works,* by Algernon Charles Swinburne;

Jonathan Cape, Limited, London, for "She Comes Not When Noon Is on the Roses" and "Come, Let Us Make Love Deathless," by Herbert Trench; and to

Mrs. William Butler Yeats, The Macmillan Company, New York, and Macmillan & Co., Ltd., London, for "When You Are Old," from *Early Poems and Stories,* by W. B. Yeats, and *Collected Poems of W. B. Yeats.*

CONTENTS

CONTENTS

[xii]

CONTENTS

[xiii]

CONTENTS

CONTENTS

HELEN OF KIRCONNELL

I wish I were where Helen lies,
Night and day on me she cries;
O that I were where Helen lies,
On fair Kirconnell Lee!

Curst be the heart that thought the thought,
And curst the hand that fired the shot,
When in my arms burd Helen dropt,
And died to succour me!

O think na ye my heart was sair,
When my love dropt down and spak nae mair!
There did she swoon wi' meikle care,
On fair Kirconnell Lee.

As I went down the water side,
None but my foe to be my guide,
None but my foe to be my guide,
On fair Kirconnell Lee;

I lighted down my sword to draw,
I hacked him in pieces sma',
I hacked him in pieces sma',
For her sake that died for me.

BALLAD

O Helen fair beyond compare,
I'll mak a garland o' thy hair,
Shall bind my heart for evermair,
Until the day I dee.

O that I were where Helen lies!
Night and day on me she cries;
Out of my bed she bids me rise,
Says, "Haste and come to me!"—

O Helen fair! O Helen chaste!
If I were with thee I were blest,
Where thou lies low, and taks thy rest,
On fair Kirconnell Lee.

I wish my grave were growing green,
A winding-sheet drawn ower my e'en,
And I in Helen's arms lying,
On fair Kirconnell Lee.

I wish I were where Helen lies!
Night and day on me she cries;
And I am weary of the skies,
For her sake that died for me.

ANNIE LAURIE

Maxwellton braes are bonnie,
  Where early fa's the dew
And it's there that Annie Laurie
  Gi'ed me her promise true;—
  Gi'ed me her promise true
Which ne'er forgot will be;
And for bonnie Annie Laurie
  I'd lay me down and dee.

Her brow is like the snawdrift,
  Her neck is like the swan,
Her face it is the fairest
  That e'er the sun shone on;—
  That e'er the sun shone on;
And dark blue is her e'e;
And for bonnie Annie Laurie
  I'd lay me down and dee.

Like dew on the gowan lying,
  Is the fa' o' her fairy feet;
And like winds in summer sighing,
  Her voice is low and sweet;—

BALLAD

Her voice is low and sweet,
And she's a' the world to me;
And for bonnie Annie Laurie
I'd lay me down and dee.

BALLAD

ON A LOST OPPORTUNITY

WE MIGHT, if you had willed, have conquered Heaven.
Once only in our lives before the gate
Of Paradise we stood, one fortunate even,
And gazed in sudden rapture through the grate.
And, while you stood astonished, I, our fate
Venturing, pushed the latch and found it free.
There stood the tree of knowledge fair and great
Beside the tree of life. One instant we
Stood in that happy garden, guardianless.
My hands already turned towards the tree
And in another moment we had known
The taste of joy and immortality
And been ourselves as gods. But in distress
You thrust me back with supplicating arms
And eyes of terror, till the impatient sun
Had time to set and till the heavenly host
Rushed forth with clarions and alarms
And cast us out for ever, blind and lost.

WILFRID SCAWEN BLUNT

[5]

ST. VALENTINE'S DAY

To-day, all day, I rode upon the down,
With hounds and horsemen, a brave company.
On this side in its glory lay the sea,
On that the Sussex weald, a sea of brown.
The wind was light, and brightly the sun shone,
And still we gallop'd on from gorse to gorse:
And once, when check'd, a thrush sang, and my horse
Prick'd his quick ears as to a sound unknown.

I knew the Spring was come. I knew it even
Better than all by this, that through my chase
In bush and stone and hill and sea and heaven
I seem'd to see and follow still your face.
Your face my quarry was. For it I rode,
My horse a thing of wings, myself a god.

WILFRID SCAWEN BLUNT

NIGHT

The night has a thousand eyes,
  And the day but one;
Yet the light of the bright world dies
  With the dying sun.

The mind has a thousand eyes,
  And the heart but one;
Yet the light of a whole life dies,
  When love is done.

FRANCIS WILLIAM BOURDILLON

WHEN DEATH TO EITHER SHALL COME

WHEN DEATH to either shall come,—
 I pray it be first to me,—
Be happy as ever at home,
 If so, as I wish, it be.

Possess thy heart, my own;
 And sing to the child on thy knee,
Or read to thyself alone
 The songs that I made for thee.

ROBERT BRIDGES

AWAKE, MY HEART

Awake, my heart, to be loved, awake, awake!
The darkness silvers away, the moon doth break,
It leaps in the sky: unrisen lustres slake
The o'ertaken moon. Awake, O heart, awake!

She too that loveth awaketh and hopes for thee;
Her eyes already have sped the shades that flee,
Already they watch the path thy feet shall take:
Awake, O heart, to be loved, awake, awake!

And if thou tarry from her,—if this could be,—
She cometh herself, O heart, to be loved, to thee;
For thee would unashamèd herself forsake:
Awake to be loved, my heart, awake, awake!

ROBERT BRIDGES

SO SWEET LOVE SEEMED

So SWEET love seemed that April morn,
When first we kissed beside the thorn,
So strangely sweet, it was not strange
We thought that love could never change.

But I can tell—let truth be told—
That love will change in growing old;
Though day by day is nought to see,
So delicate his motions be.

And in the end 'twill come to pass
Quite to forget what once he was.
Nor even in fancy to recall
The pleasure that was all in all.

His little spring, that sweet we found,
So deep in summer floods is drowned,
I wonder, bathed in joy complete,
How love so young could be so sweet.

ROBERT BRIDGES

REMEMBRANCE

COLD IN the earth—and the deep snow piled above thee
  Far, far removed, cold in the dreary grave!
Have I forgot, my only Love, to love thee,
  Sever'd at last by Time's all-severing wave?

Now, when alone, do my thoughts no longer hover
  Over the mountains, on that northern shore,
Resting their wings where heath and fern-leaves cover
  Thy noble heart for ever, ever more?

Cold in the earth—and fifteen wild Decembers
  From those brown hills have melted into spring:
Faithful, indeed, is the spirit that remembers
  After such years of change and suffering!

Sweet Love of youth, forgive, if I forget thee,
  While the world's tide is bearing me along;
Other desires and other hopes beset me,
  Hopes which obscure, but cannot do thee wrong!

No later light has lighten'd up my heaven,
  No second morn has ever shone for me;
All my life's bliss from thy dear life was given,
  All my life's bliss is in the grave with thee.

But when the days of golden dreams had perish'd,
  And even Despair was powerless to destroy;
Then did I learn how existence could be cherish'd,
  Strengthen'd, and fed, without the aid of joy.

Then did I check the tears of useless passion—
  Wean'd my young soul from yearning after thine;
Sternly denied its burning wish to hasten
  Down to that tomb already more than mine.

And, even yet, I dare not let it languish,
  Dare not indulge in mcmory's rapturous pain;
Once drinking deep of that divinest anguish,
  How could I seek the empty world again?

EMILY BRONTË

JESSIE

WHEN Jessie comes with her soft breast,
  And yields the golden keys,
Then is it as if God caress'd
  Twin babes upon His knees—
Twin babes that, each to other press'd,
Just feel the Father's arms, wherewith they both are
    bless'd.

But when I think if we must part,
  And all this personal dream be fled—
O then my heart! O then my useless heart!
  Would God that thou wert dead—
A clod insensible to joys or ills—
A stone remote in some bleak gully of the hills!

THOMAS EDWARD BROWN

SONNETS FROM THE PORTUGUESE

SONNET I

I THOUGHT once how Theocritus had sung
Of the sweet years, the dear and wish'd-for years,
Who each one in a gracious hand appears
To bear a gift for mortals old or young:
And, as I mused it in his antique tongue,
I saw in gradual vision through my tears
The sweet, sad years, the melancholy years—
Those of my own life, who by turns had flung
A shadow across me. Straightway I was 'ware,
So weeping, how a mystic Shape did move
Behind me, and drew me backward by the hair;
And a voice said in mastery, while I strove,
"Guess now who holds thee?"—"Death!" I said.
    But there
The silver answer rang— "Not Death, but Love."

ELIZABETH BARRETT BROWNING

SONNETS FROM THE PORTUGUESE

Sonnet XXII

When our two souls stand up erect and strong,
Face to face, silent, drawing nigh and nigher,
Until the lengthening wings break into fire
At either curvéd point,—what bitter wrong
Can the earth do us, that we should not long
Be here contented? Think! In mounting higher,
The angels would press on us, and aspire
To drop some golden orb of perfect song
Into our deep, dear silence. Let us stay
Rather on earth, Belovèd—where the unfit
Contrarious moods of men recoil away
And isolate pure spirits, and permit
A place to stand and love in for a day,
With darkness and the death-hour rounding it.

ELIZABETH BARRETT BROWNING

MEETING AT NIGHT

I

THE grey sea and the long black land;
And the yellow half-moon large and low;
And the startled little waves that leap
In fiery ringlets from their sleep,
As I gain the cove with pushing prow,
And quench its speed in the slushy sand.

II

Then a mile of warm sea-scented beach;
Three fields to cross till a farm appears;
A tap at the pane, the quick sharp scratch
And blue spurt of a lighted match,
And a voice less loud, thro' its joys and fears,
Than the two hearts beating each to each!

ROBERT BROWNING

PARTING AT MORNING

Round the cape of a sudden came the sea,
And the sun looked over the mountain's rim—
And straight was a path of gold for him,
And the need of a world of men for me.

ROBERT BROWNING

IN A GONDOLA

He sings.

I SEND my heart up to thee, all my heart
   In this my singing.
For the stars help me, and the sea bears part;
   The very night is clinging
Closer to Venice' streets to leave one space
   Above me, whence thy face
May light my joyous heart to thee its dwelling-
   place.

She speaks.

Say after me, and try to say
My very words, as if each word
Came from you of your own accord,
In your own voice, in your own way:
"This woman's heart and soul, and brain
"Are mine as much as this gold chain
"She bids me wear; which" (say again)
"I choose to make by cherishing
"A precious thing, or choose to fling
"Over the boat-side, ring by ring."
And yet once more say...no word more!
Since words are only words. Give o'er!

Unless you call me, all the same,
Familiarly by my pet name,
Which, if the Three should hear you call,
And me reply to, would proclaim
At once our secret to them all.
Ask of me, too, command me, blame—
Do break down the partition-wall
'Twixt us, the daylight world beholds
Curtained in dusk and splendid folds.
What's left but—all of me to take?
I am the Three's; prevent them, slake
Your thirst! 'Tis said, the Arab sage,
In practising with gems, can loose
Their subtle spirit in his cruce
And leave but ashes: so, sweet mage,
Leave them my ashes when thy use
Sucks out my soul, thy heritage!

He sings.

I

Past we glide, and past, and past!
   What's that poor Agnese doing
Where they make the shutters fast?
   Grey Zanobi's just a-wooing
To his couch the purchased bride:
   Past we glide!

II

Past we glide, and past, and past!
  Why's the Pucci Palace flaring
Like a beacon to the blast?
  Guests by hundreds, not one caring
If the dear host's neck were wried:
  Past we glide!

She sings.

I

The Moth's kiss, first!
Kiss me as if you made believe
You were not sure, this eve,
How my face, your flower, had pursed
Its petals up; so, here and there,
You brush it, till I grow aware
Who wants me, and wide ope I burst.

II

The Bee's kiss, now!
Kiss me as if you entered gay
My heart at some noonday,
A bud that dares not disallow
The claim, so all is rendered up,
And passively its shattered cup
Over your head to sleep I bow.

ROBERT BROWNING

He sings.

I

What are we two?
I am a Jew,
And carry thee, farther than friends can pursue,
To a feast of our tribe;
Where they need thee to bribe
The devil that blasts them unless he imbibe
Thy...Scatter the vision for ever! And now,
As of old, I am I, thou art thou!

II

Say again, what are we?
The sprite of a star,
I lure thee above where the Destinies bar
My plumes their full play
Till a ruddier ray
Than my pale one announce there is withering
    away
Some...Scatter the vision for ever! And now,
As of old, I am I, thou art thou!

He muses.

Oh, which were best, to roam or rest?
The land's lap or the water's breast?
To sleep on yellow millet-sheaves,

Or swim in lucid shallows just
Eluding water-lily leaves,
An inch from Death's black fingers, thrust
To lock you, whom release he must;
Which life were best on Summer eves?

He speaks, musing.

Lie back; could thought of mine improve you?
From this shoulder let there spring
A wing; from this, another wing;
Wings, not legs and feet, shall move you!
Snow-white must they spring, to blend
With your flesh, but I intend
They shall deepen to the end,
Broader, into burning gold,
Till both wings crescent-wise enfold
Your perfect self, from 'neath your feet
To o'er your head, where, lo! they meet
As if a million sword-blades hurled
Defiance from you to the world!

Rescue me thou, the only real!
And scare away this mad ideal
That came, nor motions to depart!
Thanks! Now, stay ever as thou art!

ROBERT BROWNING

Still he muses.

I

What if the Three should catch at last
Thy serenader? While there's cast
Paul's cloak about my head, and fast
Gian pinions me, Himself has past
His stylet thro' my back; I reel;
And...is it thou I feel?

II

They trail me, these three godless knaves,
Past every church that saints and saves,
Nor stop till, where the cold sea raves
By Lido's wet accursed graves,
They scoop mine, roll me to its brink,
And...on thy breast I sink!

She replies, musing.

Dip your arm o'er the boat-side, elbow-deep,
As I do: thus: were Death so unlike sleep,
Caught this way? Death's to fear from flame, or
  steel,
Or poison doubtless; but from water—feel!

Go find the bottom! Would you stay me? There!
Now pluck a great blade of that ribbon-grass
To plait in where the foolish jewel was,
I flung away; since you have praised my hair,
'Tis proper to be choice in what I wear.

He speaks.

Row home? must we row home? Too surely
Know I where its front's demurely
Over the Giudecca piled;
Window just with window mating,
Door on door exactly waiting,
All's the set face of a child:
But, behind it, where's a trace
Of the staidness and reserve,
And formal lines without a curve,
In the same child's playing-face?
No two windows look one way
O'er the small sea-water thread
Below them. Ah, the autumn day
I, passing, saw you overhead!
First, out a cloud of curtain blew,
Then a sweet cry, and last came you—
To catch your lory that must needs
Escape just then, of all times then,
To peck a tall plant's fleecy seeds,
And make me happiest of men.

[24]

I scarce could breathe to see you reach
So far back o'er the balcony
To catch him ere he climbed too high
Above you in the Smyrna peach
That quick the round smooth cord of gold,
This coiled hair on your head, unrolled,
Fell down you like a gorgeous snake
The Roman girls were wont, of old,
When Rome there was, for coolness' sake
To let lie curling o'er their bosoms.
Dear lory, may his beak retain
Ever its delicate rose stain
As if the wounded lotus-blossoms
Had marked their thief to know again!

Stay longer yet, for others' sake
Than mine! What should your chamber do?
—With all its rarities that ache
In silence while day lasts, but wake
At night-time and their life renew,
Suspended just to pleasure you
Who brought against their will together
These objects, and, while day lasts, weave
Around them such a magic tether
That they look dumb: your harp, believe,
With all the sensitive tight strings
That dare not speak, now to itself
Breathes slumbrously as if some elf

Went in and out the chords, his wings
Make murmur wheresoe'er they graze,
As an angel may, between the maze
Of midnight palace-pillars, on
And on, to sow God's plagues, have gone
Through guilty glorious Babylon.
And while such murmurs flow, the nymph
Bends o'er the harp-top from her shell
As the dry limpet for the lymph
Come with a tune he knows so well.
And how your statues' hearts must swell!
And how your pictures must descend
To see each other, friend with friend!
Oh, could you take them by surprise,
You'd find Schidone's eager Duke
Doing the quaintest courtesies
To that prim Saint by Haste-thee-Luke:
And, deeper into her rock den,
Bold Castelfranco's Magdalen
You'd find retreated from the ken
Of that robed counsel-keeping Ser—
As if the Tizian thinks of her,
And is not, rather, gravely bent
On seeing for himself what toys
Are these, his progeny invent,
What litter now the board employs
Whereon he signed a document
That got him murdered! Each enjoys

Its night so well, you cannot break
The sport up so, indeed must make
More stay with me, for others' sake.

She speaks.

I

To-morrow, if a harp-string, say,
Is used to tie the jasmine back
That overfloods my room with sweets,
Contrive your Zorzi somehow meets
My Zanze! if the ribbon's black,
The Three are watching: keep away!

II

Your gondola—let Zorzi wreathe
A mesh of water-weeds about
Its prow, as if he unaware
Had struck some quay or bridge-foot stair;
That I may throw a paper out
As you and he go underneath.

There's Zanze's vigilant taper; safe are we.
Only one minute more to-night with me?
Resume your past self of a month ago!
Be you the bashful gallant, I will be
The lady with the colder breast than snow:

Now bow you, as becomes, nor touch my hand
More than I touch yours when I step to land,
And say, "All thanks, Siora!"—
                              Heart to heart,
And lips to lips! Yet once more, ere we part,
Clasp me and make me thine, as mine thou art!

He is surprised, and stabbed.

It was ordained to be so, sweet,—and best
Comes now, beneath thine eyes, upon thy breast.
Still kiss me! Care not for the cowards! Care
Only to put aside thy beauteous hair
My blood will hurt! The Three, I do not scorn
To death, because they never lived: but I
Have lived indeed, and so—(yet one more kiss)—
    can die!

ROBERT BROWNING

A LOVERS' QUARREL

OH, WHAT a dawn of day!
How the March sun feels like May!
    All is blue again
    After last night's rain,
And the South dries the hawthorn-spray.
    Only, my Love's away!
I'd as lief that the blue were grey.

Runnels, which rillets swell,
Must be dancing down the dell,
    With a foaming head
    On the beryl bed
Paven as smooth as a hermit's cell;
    Each with a tale to tell,
Could my Love but attend as well.

Dearest, three months ago!
When we lived blocked-up with snow,—
    When the wind would edge
    In and in his wedge,
In, as far as the point could go—
    Not to our ingle, though,
Where we loved each the other so!

Laughs with so little cause!
We devised games out of straws.
    We would try and trace
    One another's face
In the ash, as an artist draws;
    Free on each other's flaws,
How we chattered like two church daws!

What's in the "Times"?—a scold
At the emperor deep and cold;
    He has taken a bride
    To his gruesome side,
That's as fair as himself is bold:
    There they sit ermine-stoled,
And she powders her hair with gold.

Fancy the Pampas' sheen!
Miles and miles of gold and green
    Where the sunflowers blow
    In a solid glow,
And—to break now and then the screen—
    Black neck and eyeballs keen,
Up a wild horse leaps between!

Try, will our table turn?
Lay your hands there light, and yearn
    Till the yearning slips
    Thro' the finger tips

In a fire which few discern,
   And a very few feel burn,
And the rest, they may live and learn!

Then we two would up and pace,
For a change, about the place,
   Each with arm o'er neck:
   'Tis our quarter-deck,
We are seamen in woeful case.
   Help in the ocean-space!
Or, if no help, we'll embrace.

See, how she looks now, dressed
In a sledging-cap and vest!
   'Tis a huge fur cloak—
   Like a reindeer's yoke
Falls the lappet along the breast:
   Sleeves for her arms to rest,
Or to hang, as my Love likes best.

Teach me to flirt a fan
As the Spanish ladies can,
   Or I tint your lip
   With a burnt stick's tip
And you turn into such a man!
   Just the two spots that span
Half the bill of a young male swan.

[31]

Dearest, three months ago
When the mesmeriser Snow
    With his hand's first sweep
    Put the earth to sleep:
'Twas a time when the heart could show
    All—how was earth to know,
'Neath the mute hand's to-and-fro?

Dearest, three months ago
When we loved each other so,
    Lived and loved the same
    Till an evening came
When a shaft from the devil's bow
    Pierced to our ingle-glow,
And the friends were friend and foe!

Not from the heart beneath—
'Twas a bubble born of breath,
    Neither sneer nor vaunt,
    Nor reproach nor taunt.
See a word, how it severeth!
    Oh, the power of life and death
In the tongue, as the Preacher saith!

Woman, and will you cast
For a word, quite off at last
    Me, your own, your You,—
    Since, as truth is true,

ROBERT BROWNING

I was You all the happy past—
    Me do you leave aghast
With the memories We amassed?

Love, if you knew the light
That your soul casts in my sight,
    How I look to you
    For the pure and true
And the beauteous and the right,—
    Bear with a moment's spite
When a mere mote threats the white!

What of a hasty word?
Is the fleshly heart not stirred
    By a worm's pin-prick
    Where its roots are quick?
See the eye, by a fly's foot blurred—
    Ear, when a straw is heard
Scratch the brain's coat of curd!

Foul be the world or fair
More or less, how can I care?
    'Tis the world the same
    For my praise or blame,
And endurance is easy there.
    Wrong in the one thing rare—
Oh, it is hard to bear!

Here's the spring back or close,
When the almond-blossom blows:
    We shall have the word
    In a minor third
There is none but the cuckoo knows:
    Heaps of the guelder-rose!
I must bear with it, I suppose.

Could but November come,
Were the noisy birds struck dumb
    At the warning slash
    Of his driver's-lash—
I would laugh like the valiant Thumb
    Facing the castle glum
And the giant's fee-faw-fum!

Then, were the world well stripped
Of the gear wherein equipped
    We can stand apart,
    Heart dispense with heart
In the sun, with the flowers unnipped,—
    Oh, the world's hangings ripped,
We were both in a bare-walled crypt!

Each in the crypt would cry
"But one freezes here! and why?
    When a heart, as chill,
    At my own would thrill

Back to life, and its fires out-fly?
Heart, shall we live or die?
The rest, ... settle it by and by!"

So, she'd efface the score,
And forgive me as before.
It is twelve o'clock:
I shall hear her knock
In the worst of a storm's uproar,
I shall pull her through the door,
I shall have her for evermore!

ROBERT BROWNING

ANY WIFE TO ANY HUSBAND

M Y LOVE, this is the bitterest, that thou
Who art all truth and who dost love me now
 As thine eyes say, as thy voice breaks to say—
Should'st love so truly and could'st love me still
A whole long life through, had but love its will,
 Would death that leads me from thee brook delay!

I have but to be by thee, and thy hand
Would never let mine go, thy heart withstand
 The beating of my heart to reach its place.
When should I look for thee and feel thee gone?
When cry for the old comfort and find none?
 Never, I know! Thy soul is in thy face.

Oh, I should fade—'tis willed so! might I save,
Gladly I would, whatever beauty gave
 Joy to thy sense, for that was precious too.
It is not to be granted. But the soul
Whence the love comes, all ravage leaves that whole;
 Vainly the flesh fades—soul makes all things new.

And 'twould not be because my eye grew dim
Thou could'st not find the love there, thanks to Him

Who never is dishonoured in the spark
He gave us from his fire of fires, and bade
Remember whence it sprang nor be afraid
   While that burns on, though all the rest grow dark.

So, how thou would'st be perfect, white and clean
Outside as inside, soul and soul's demesne
   Alike, this body given to show it by!
Oh, three-parts through the worst of life's abyss,
What plaudits from the next world after this,
   Could'st thou repeat a stroke and gain the sky!

And is it not the bitterer to think
That, disengage our hands and thou wilt sink
   Although thy love was love in very deed?
I know that nature! Pass a festive day
Thou dost not throw its relic-flower away
   Nor bid its music's loitering echo speed.

Thou let'st the stranger's glove lie where it fell;
If old things remain old things all is well,
   For thou art grateful as becomes man best:
And hadst thou only heard me play one tune,
Or viewed me from a window, not so soon
   With thee would such things fade as with the rest.

I seem to see! we meet and part: 'tis brief:
The book I opened keeps a folded leaf,
   The very chair I sat on, breaks the rank;

[37]

That is a portrait of me on the wall—
Three lines, my face comes at so slight a call;
    And for all this, one little hour's to thank.

But now, because the hour through years was fixed,
Because our inmost beings met and mixed,
    Because thou once hast loved me—wilt thou dare
Say to thy soul and Who may list beside,
"Therefore she is immortally my bride,
    Chance cannot change that love, nor time impair.

"So, what if in the dusk of life that's left,
I, a tired traveller, of my sun bereft,
    Look from my path when, mimicking the same,
The fire-fly glimpses past me, come and gone?
—Where was it till the sunset? where anon
    It will be at the sunrise! what's to blame?"

Is it so helpful to thee? canst thou take
The mimic up, nor, for the true thing's sake,
    Put gently by such efforts at a beam?
Is the remainder of the way so long
Thou need'st the little solace, thou the strong?
    Watch out thy watch, let weak ones doze and dream!

—Ah, but the fresher faces! "Is it true,
Thou'lt ask, "some eyes are beautiful and new?
    Some hair,—how can one choose but grasp such wealth?

And if a man should press his lips to lips
Fresh as the wilding hedge-rose-cup there slips
   The dew-drop out of, must it be by stealth?

"It cannot change the love still kept for Her,
More than if such a picture I prefer
   Passing a day with, to a room's bare side.
The painted form takes nothing she possessed,
Yet while the Titian's Venus lies at rest
   A man looks. Once more, what is there to chide?"

So must I see, from where I sit and watch,
My own self sell myself, my hand attach
   Its warrant to the very thefts from me—
Thy singleness of soul that made me proud,
Thy purity of heart I loved aloud,
   Thy man's truth I was bold to bid God see!

Love so, then, if thou wilt! Give all thou canst
Away to the new faces—disentranced—
   (Say it and think it) obdurate no more,
Re-issue looks and words from the old mint—
Pass them afresh, no matter whose the print
   Image and superscription once they bore!

Re-coin thyself and give it them to spend,—
It all comes to the same thing at the end,
   Since mine thou wast, mine art, and mine shalt be,

Faithful or faithless, sealing up the sum
Or lavish of my treasure, thou must come
　　Back to the heart's place here I keep for thee!

Only, why should it be with stain at all?
Why must I, 'twixt the leaves of coronal,
　　Put any kiss of pardon on thy brow?
Why need the other women know so much
And talk together, "Such the look and such
　　The smile he used to love with, then as now!"

Might I die last and show thee! Should I find
Such hardship in the few years left behind,
　　If free to take and light my lamp, and go
Into thy tomb, and shut the door and sit
Seeing thy face on those four sides of it
　　The better that they are so blank, I know!

Why, time was what I wanted, to turn o'er
Within my mind each look, get more and more
　　By heart each word, too much to learn at first,
And join thee all the fitter for the pause
'Neath the low doorway's lintel. That were cause
　　For lingering, though thou calledst, if I durst!

And yet thou art the nobler of us two.
What dare I dream of, that thou canst not do,
　　Outstripping my ten small steps with one stride?

I'll say then, here's a trial and a task—
Is it to bear?—if easy, I'll not ask—
  Though love fail, I can trust on in my pride.

Pride?—when those eyes forestall the life behind
The death I have to go through!—when I find
  Now that I want thy help most, all of thee!
What did I fear? Thy love shall hold me fast
Until the little minute's sleep is past
  And I wake saved.—And yet, it will not be!

ROBERT BROWNING

LOVE AMONG THE RUINS

I

Where the quiet-coloured end of evening smiles
    Miles and miles
On the solitary pastures where our sheep
    Half-asleep
Tinkle homeward thro' the twilight, stray or stop
    As they crop—
Was the site once of a city great and gay,
    (So they say)
Of our country's very capital, its prince
    Ages since
Held his court in, gathered councils, wielding far
    Peace or war.

II

Now—the country does not even boast a tree
    As you see,
To distinguish slopes of verdure, certain rills
    From the hills
Intersect and give a name to, (else they run
    Into one)

[42]

Where the domed and daring palace shot its spires
    Up like fires
O'er the hundred-gated circuit of a wall
    Bounding all,
Made of marble, men might march on nor be prest,
    Twelve abreast.

III

And such plenty and perfection, see, of grass
    Never was!
Such a carpet as, this summer-time, o'erspreads
    And embeds
Every vestige of the city, guessed alone,
    Stock or stone—
Where a multitude of men breathed joy and woe
    Long ago;
Lust of glory pricked their hearts up, dread of shame
    Struck them tame;
And that glory and that shame alike, the gold
    Bought and sold.

IV

Now,—the single little turret that remains
    On the plains,
By the caper overrooted, by the gourd
    Overscored,

While the patching houseleek's head of blossom winks
    Through the chinks—
Marks the basement whence a tower in ancient time
    Sprang sublime,
And a burning ring, all round, the chariots traced
    As they raced,
And the monarch and his minions and his dames
    Viewed the games.

V

And I know, while thus the quiet-coloured eve
    Smiles to leave
To their folding, all our many-tinkling fleece
    In such peace,
And the slopes and rills in undistinguished grey
    Melt away—
That a girl with eager eyes and yellow hair
    Waits me there
In the turret, whence the charioteers caught soul
    For the goal,
When the king looked, where she looks now, breathless,
dumb
    Till I come.

VI

But he looked upon the city, every side,
    Far and wide,

All the mountains topped with temples, all the glades'
    Colonnades,
All the causeys, bridges, aqueducts,—and then,
    All the men!
When I do come, she will speak not, she will stand,
    Either hand
On my shoulder, give her eyes the first embrace
    Of my face,
Ere we rush, ere we extinguish sight and speech
    Each on each.

VII

In one year they sent a million fighters forth
    South and north,
And they built their gods a brazen pillar high
    As the sky,
Yet reserved a thousand chariots in full force—
    Gold, of course.
Oh, heart! oh blood that freezes, blood that burns!
    Earth's returns
For whole centuries of folly, noise and sin!
    Shut them in,
With their triumphs and their glories and the rest.
    Love is best!

ROBERT BROWNING

IN THREE DAYS

So, I SHALL see her in three days
And just one night, but nights are short,
Then two long hours, and that is morn.
See how I come, unchanged, unworn!
Feel, where my life broke off from thine,
How fresh the splinters keep and fine,—
Only a touch, and we combine!

Too long, this time of year, the days!
But nights—at least the nights are short.
As night shows where her one moon is,
A hand's-breadth of pure light and bliss,
So, life's night gives my lady birth
And my eyes hold her! What is worth
The rest of heaven, the rest of earth?

O loaded curls, release your store
Of warmth and scent, as once before
The tingling hair did, lights and darks
Out-breaking into fairy sparks,
When under curl and curl I pried
After the warmth and scent inside,

Thro' lights and darks how manifold—
The dark inspired, the light controlled!
As early Art embrowns the gold.

What great fear, should one say, "Three days
That change the world might change as well
Your fortune; and if joy delays,
Be happy that no worse befell."
What small fear, if another says,
"Three days and one short night beside
May throw no shadow on your ways;
But years must teem with change untried,
With chance not easily defied,
With an end somewhere undescried."
No fear!—or if a fear be born
This minute, it dies out in scorn.
Fear? I shall see her in three days
And one night, now the nights are short,
Then just two hours, and that is morn.

ROBERT BROWNING

TWO IN THE CAMPAGNA

I WONDER do you feel to-day
  As I have felt, since, hand in hand,
We sat down on the grass, to stray
  In spirit better through the land,
This morn of Rome and May?

For me, I touched a thought, I know,
  Has tantalised me many times,
(Like turns of thread the spiders throw
  Mocking across our path) for rhymes
To catch at and let go.

Help me to hold it: first it left
  The yellowing fennel, run to seed
There, branching from the brickwork's cleft,
  Some old tomb's ruin: yonder weed
Took up the floating weft,

Where one small orange cup amassed
  Five beetles,—blind and green they grope
Among the honey-meal: and last
  Everywhere on the grassy slope
I traced it. Hold it fast!

The champaign with its endless fleece
  Of feathery grasses everywhere!
Silence and passion, joy and peace,
  An everlasting wash of air—
Rome's ghost since her decease.

Such life there, through such lengths of hours,
  Such miracles performed in play,
Such primal naked forms of flowers,
  Such letting Nature have her way
While Heaven looks from its towers.

How say you? Let us, O my dove,
  Let us be unashamed of soul,
As earth lies bare to heaven above!
  How is it under our control
To love or not to love?

I would that you were all to me,
  You that are just so much, no more—
Nor yours, nor mine,—nor slave, nor free!
  Where does the fault lie? what the core
Of the wound, since wound must be?

I would I could adopt your will,
  See with your eyes, and set my heart
Beating by yours, and drink my fill
  At your soul's springs,—your part, my part
In life, for good and ill.

No. I yearn upward—touch you close,
   Then stand away. I kiss your cheek,
Catch your soul's warmth,—I pluck the rose
   And love it more than tongue can speak—
Then the good minute goes.

Already how am I so far
   Out of that minute? Must I go
Still like the thistle-ball, no bar,
   Onward, whenever light winds blow,
Fixed by no friendly star?

Just when I seemed about to learn!
   Where is the thread now? Off again!
The old trick! Only I discern—
   Infinite passion and the pain
Of finite hearts that yearn.

ROBERT BROWNING

MISCONCEPTIONS

I

THIS IS a spray the Bird clung to,
　　Making it blossom with pleasure,
Ere the high tree-top she sprung to,
　　Fit for her nest and her treasure.
　　Oh, what a hope beyond measure
Was the poor spray's, which the flying feet hung to,—
So to be singled out, built in, and sung to!

II

This is a heart the Queen leant on,
　　Thrilled in a moment erratic,
Ere the true bosom she bent on,
　　Meet for love's regal dalmatic.
　　Oh, what a fancy ecstatic
Was the poor heart's, ere the wanderer went on—
Love to be saved for it, proffered to, spent on!

ROBERT BROWNING

"O LYRIC LOVE..."

From THE RING AND THE BOOK

O LYRIC LOVE, half angel and half bird
And all a wonder and a wild desire,—
Boldest of hearts that ever braved the sun,
Took sanctuary within the holier blue,
And sang a kindred soul out to his face,—
Yet human at the red-ripe of the heart—
When the first summons from the darkling earth
Reached thee amid thy chambers, blanched their blue,
And bared them of their glory,—to drop down,
To toil for man, to suffer or to die,—
This is the same voice: can thy soul know change?
Hail then, and hearken from the realms of help!
Never may I commence my song, my due
To God who best taught song by gift of thee,
Except with bent head and beseeching hand—
That still, despite the distance and the dark,
What was, again may be; some interchange
Of grace, some splendour once thy very thought,
Some benediction anciently thy smile:
—Never conclude, but raising hand and head
Thither where eyes, that cannot reach, yet yearn

For all hope, all sustainment, all reward,
Their utmost up and on,—so blessing back
In those thy realms of help, that heaven thy home,
Some whiteness which, I judge, thy face makes proud,
Some wanness where, I think, thy foot may fall!

ROBERT BROWNING

JAMES LEE'S WIFE

On Deck

There is nothing to remember in me,
  Nothing I ever said with a grace,
Nothing I did that you cared to see,
  Nothing I was that deserves a place
In your mind, now I leave you, set you free.

Conceded! In turn, concede to me,
  Such things have been as a mutual flame.
Your soul's locked fast; but, love for a key,
  You might let it loose, till I grew the same
In your eyes, as in mine you stand: strange plea!

For then, then, what would it matter to me
  That I was the harsh, ill-favoured one?
We both should be like as pea and pea;
  It was ever so since the world begun:
So, let me proceed with my reverie.

How strange it were if you had all me,
  As I have all you in my heart and brain,

ROBERT BROWNING

You, whose least word brought gloom or glee,
  Who never lifted the hand in vain—
Will hold mine yet, from over the sea!

Strange, if a face, when you thought of me,
  Rose like your own face present now,
With eyes as dear in their due degree,
  Much such a mouth, and as bright a brow,
Till you saw yourself, while you cried, " 'Tis She!"

Well, you may, you must, set down to me
  Love that was life, life that was love;
A tenure of breath at your lips' decree,
  A passion to stand as your thoughts approve,
A rapture to fall where your foot might be.

But did one touch of such love for me
  Come in a word or a look of yours,
Whose words and looks will, circling, flee
  Round me and round while life endures—
Could I fancy, "As I feel, thus feels he";

Why, fade you might to a thing like me,
  And your hair grow these coarse hanks of hair,
And your skin, this bark of a gnarled tree,—
  You might turn myself!—should I know or care
When I should be dead of joy, James Lee?

ROBERT BROWNING

[55]

ONE WORD MORE

To E.B.B.

1855

THERE they are, my fifty men and women
Naming me the fifty poems finished!
Take them, Love, the book and me together.
Where the heart lies, let the brain lie also.

Rafael made a century of sonnets,
Made and wrote them in a certain volume
Dinted with the silver-pointed pencil
Else he only used to draw Madonnas:
These, the world might view—but one, the volume.
Who that one, you ask? Your heart instructs you.
Did she live and love it all her life-time?
Did she drop, his lady of the sonnets,
Die, and let it drop beside her pillow
Where it lay in place of Rafael's glory,
Rafael's cheek so duteous and so loving—
Cheek, the world was wont to hail a painter's,
Rafael's cheek, her love had turned a poet's?

ROBERT BROWNING

You and I would rather read that volume,
(Taken to his beating bosom by it)
Lean and list the bosom-beats of Rafael,
Would we not? than wonder at Madonnas—
Her, San Sisto names, and Her, Foligno,
Her, that visits Florence in a vision,
Her, that's left with lilies in the Louvre—
Seen by us and all the world in circle.

You and I will never read that volume.
Guido Reni, like his own eye's apple
Guarded long the treasure-book and loved it.
Guido Reni dying, all Bologna
Cried, and the world cried too, "Ours—the treasure!"
Suddenly, as rare things will, it vanished.

Dante once prepared to paint an angel:
Whom to please? You whisper "Beatrice."
While he mused and traced it and retraced it,
(Peradventure with a pen corroded
Still by drops of that hot ink he dipped for,
When, his left hand i' the hair o' the wicked,
Back he held the brow and pricked its stigma,
Bit into the live man's flesh for parchment,
Loosed him, laughed to see the writing rankle,
Let the wretch go festering through Florence)—
Dante, who loved well because he hated,
Hated wickedness that hinders loving,

[57]

Dante, standing, studying his angel,—
In there broke the folk of his Inferno.
Says he—"Certain people of importance"
(Such he gave his daily dreadful line to)
"Entered, and would seize, forsooth, the poet."
Says the poet—"Then I stopped my painting."

You and I would rather see that angel,
Painted by the tenderness of Dante,
Would we not?—than read a fresh Inferno.

You and I will never see that picture.
While he mused on love and Beatrice,
While he softened o'er his outlined angel,
In they broke, those "people of importance:"
We and Bice bear the loss forever.

What of Rafael's sonnets, Dante's picture?

This: no artist lives and loves, that longs not
Once, and only once, and for one only,
(Ah, the prize!) to find his love a language
Fit and fair and simple and sufficient—
Using nature that's an art to others,
Not, this one time, art that's turned his nature.
Ay, of all the artists living, loving,
None but would forego his proper dowry,—
Does he paint? he fain would write a poem,—
Does he write? he fain would paint a picture,

Put to proof art alien to the artist's,
Once, and only once, and for one only,
So to be the man and leave the artist,
Gain the man's joy, miss the artist's sorrow.

Wherefore? Heaven's gift takes earth's abatement!
He who smites the rock and spreads the water,
Bidding drink and live a crowd beneath him,
Even he, the minute makes immortal,
Proves, perchance, but mortal in the minute,
Desecrates, belike, the deed in doing.
While he smites, how can he but remember,
So he smote before, in such a peril,
When they stood and mocked—"Shall smiting help us?"
When they drank and sneered—"A stroke is easy!"
When they wiped their mouths and went their journey,
Throwing him for thanks—"but drought was pleasant."
Thus old memories mar the actual triumph;
Thus the doing savours of disrelish;
Thus achievement lacks a gracious somewhat;
O'er-importuned brows becloud the mandate,
Carelessness or consciousness—the gesture.
For he bears an ancient wrong about him,
Sees and knows again those phalanxed faces,
Hears, yet one time more, the 'customed prelude—
"How shouldst thou, of all men, smite and save us?"
Guesses what is like to prove the sequel—
"Egypt's flesh-pots—nay, the drought was better."

Oh, the crowd must have emphatic warrant!
Theirs, the Sinai-forehead's cloven brilliance,
Right-arm's rod-sweep, tongue's imperial fiat.
Never dares the man put off the prophet.

Did he love one face from out the thousands,
(Were she Jethro's daughter, white and wifely,
Were she but the Æthiopian bondslave,)
He would envy yon dumb patient camel,
Keeping a reserve of scanty water,
Meant to save his own life in the desert;
Ready in the desert to deliver
(Kneeling down to let his breast be opened)
Hoard and life together for his mistress.

I shall never, in the years remaining,
Paint you pictures, no, nor carve you statues,
Make you music that would all-express me;
So it seems; I stand on my attainment.
This of verse alone, one life allows me;
Verse and nothing else have I to give you.
Other heights in other lives, God willing:
All the gifts from all the heights, your own, Love!

Yet a semblance of resource avails us—
Shade so finely touched, love's sense must seize it.
Take these lines, look lovingly and nearly,
Lines I write the first time and the last time.
He who works in fresco, steals a hair-brush,

Curbs the liberal hand, subservient proudly,
Cramps his spirit, crowds it all in little,
Makes a strange art of an art familiar,
Fills his lady's missal-marge with flowerets.
He who blows thro' bronze, may breathe thro' silver,
Fitly serenade a slumbrous princess.
He who writes, may write for once, as I do.

Love, you saw me gather men and women,
Live or dead or fashioned by my fancy,
Enter each and all, and use their service,
Speak from every mouth,—the speech, a poem.
Hardly shall I tell my joys and sorrows,
Hopes and fears, belief and disbelieving:
I am mine and yours—the rest be all men's,
Karshish, Cleon, Norbert and the fifty.
Let me speak for once in my true person,
Not as Lippo, Roland or Andrea,
Though the fruit of speech be just this sentence:
Pray you, look on these my men and women,
Take and keep my fifty poems finished;
Where my heart lies, let my brain lie also!
Poor the speech; be how I speak, for all things.

Not but that you know me! Lo, the moon's self!
Here in London, yonder late in Florence,
Still we find her face, the thrice-transfigured,
Curving on a sky imbrued with color,

Drifting over Fiesole by twilight,
Came she, our new crescent of a hair's-breadth.
Full she flared it, lamping Samminiato,
Rounder 'twixt the cypresses and rounder,
Perfect till the nightingales applauded.
Now, a piece of her old self, impoverished,
Hard to greet, she traverses the houseroofs,
Hurries with unhandsome thrift of silver,
Goes dispiritedly, glad to finish.

What, there's nothing in the moon note-worthy?
Nay: for if that moon could love a mortal,
Use, to charm him, (so to fit a fancy)
All her magic ('tis the sweet old mythos)
She would turn a new side to her mortal,
Side unseen of herdsman, huntsman, steersman—
Blank to Zoroaster on his terrace,
Blind to Galileo on his turret,
Dumb to Homer, dumb to Keats—him, even!
Think, the wonder of the moonstruck mortal—
When she turns round, comes again in heaven,
Opens out anew for worse or better!
Proves she like some portent of an iceberg
Swimming full upon the ship it founders,
Hungry with huge teeth of splintered crystals?
Proves she as the paved-work of a sapphire
Seen by Moses when he climbed the mountain?
Moses, Aaron, Nadab and Abihu

Climbed and saw the very God, the Highest
Stand upon the paved-work of a sapphire.
Shone the stone, the sapphire of that paved-work,
When they ate and drank and saw God also!

What was seen? None knows, none ever shall know.
Only this is sure—the sight were other,
Not the moon's same side, born late in Florence,
Dying now impoverished here in London.
God be thanked, the meanest of his creatures
Boasts two soul-sides, one to face the world with,
One to show a woman when he loves her!

This I say of me, but think of you, Love!
This to you—yourself my moon of poets!
Ah, but that's the world's side, there's the wonder,
Thus they see you, praise you, think they know you!
There, in turn I stand with them and praise you—
Out of my own self, I dare to phrase it.
But the best is when I glide out from them,
Cross a step or two in dubious twilight,
Come out on the other side, the novel
Silent silver lights and darks undreamed of,
Where I hush and bless myself with silence.

Oh, their Rafael of the dear Madonnas,
Oh, their Dante of the dread Inferno,
Wrote one song—and in my brain I sing it,
Drew one angel—borne, see, on my bosom.

ROBERT BROWNING

NEVER THE TIME AND THE PLACE

Never the time and the place
  And the loved one all together!
This path—how soft to pace!
  This May—what magic weather!
Where is the loved one's face?
In a dream that loved one's face meets mine,
  But the house is narrow, the place is bleak
Where, outside, rain and wind combine
  With a furtive ear, if I strive to speak,
  With a hostile eye at my flushing cheek,
With a malice that marks each word, each sign!
O enemy sly and serpentine,
  Uncoil thee from the waking man!
    Do I hold the Past
    Thus firm and fast
  Yet doubt that the Future hold I can?
This path so soft to pace shall lead
Thro' the magic of May to herself indeed!
Or narrow if needs the house must be,
Outside are the storms and the strangers: we—
Oh, close, safe, warm sleep I and she,
    —I and she!

ROBERT BROWNING

AE FOND KISS

AE FOND kiss, and then we sever;
Ae fareweel, alas, for ever!
Deep in heart-wrung tears I'll pledge thee!
Warring sighs and groans I'll wage thee!

Who shall say that fortune grieves him
While the star of hope she leaves him?
Me, nae cheerfu' twinkle lights me,
Dark despair around benights me.

I'll ne'er blame my partial fancy;
Naething could resist my Nancy;
But to see her was to love her,
Love but her, and love for ever.

Had we never lov'd sae kindly,
Had we never lov'd sae blindly,
Never met—or never parted,
We had ne'er been broken-hearted.

ROBERT BURNS

Fare thee weel, thou first and fairest!
Fare thee weel, thou best and dearest!
Thine be ilka joy and treasure,
Peace, enjoyment, love, and pleasure!

Ae fond kiss, and then we sever!
Ae fareweel, alas! for ever!
Deep in heart-wrung tears I'll pledge thee,
Warring sighs and groans I'll wage thee.

ROBERT BURNS

A RED, RED ROSE

O MY luve's like a red, red rose
    That's newly sprung in June:
O my luve's like the melodie
    That's sweetly played in tune!

As fair art thou, my bonnie lass,
    So deep in luve am I:
And I will luve thee still, my dear,
    Till a' the seas gang dry:

Till a' the seas gang dry, my dear,
    And the rocks melt wi' the sun;
And I will luve thee still, my dear,
    While the sands o' life shall run.

And fare thee weel, my only luve!
    And fare thee weel a while!
And I will come again, my luve,
    Tho' it were ten thousand mile.

ROBERT BURNS

FOLLOW YOUR SAINT

Follow your saint, follow with accents sweet!
Haste you, sad notes, fall at her flying feet!
There, wrapped in cloud of sorrow, pity move,
And tell the ravisher of my soul I perish for her love:
But if she scorns my never-ceasing pain,
Then burst with sighing in her sight, and ne'er return
    again!

All that I sung still to her praise did tend;
Still she was first; still she my songs did end;
Yet she my love and music both doth fly,
The music that her echo is and beauty's sympathy:
Then let my notes pursue her scornful flight!
It shall suffice that they were breathed and died for her
    delight.

THOMAS CAMPION

CATULLIAN HENDECASYLLABLES

Hᴇᴀʀ, my beloved, an old Milesian story!—
High, and embosom'd in congregated laurels,
Glimmer'd a temple upon a breezy headland;
In the dim distance amid the skiey billows
Rose a fair island; the god of flocks had blest it.
From the far shores of the bleak resounding island
Oft by the moonlight a little boat came floating,
Came to the sea-cave beneath the breezy headland,
Where amid myrtles a pathway stole in mazes
Up to the groves of the high embosom'd temple.
There in a thicket of dedicated roses,
Oft did a priestess, as lovely as a vision,
Pouring her soul to the son of Cytherea,
Pray him to hover around the slight canoe boat,
And with invisible pilotage to guide it
Over the dusk wave, until the nightly sailor
Shivering with ecstasy sank upon her bosom.

SAMUEL TAYLOR COLERIDGE

NON NOBIS

Not unto us, O Lord,
Not unto us the rapture of the day,
The peace of night, or love's divine surprise,
High heart, high speech, high deeds, 'mid honouring
    eyes;
For at Thy word
All these are taken away.

Not unto us, O Lord;
To us Thou givest the scorn, the scourge, the scar,
The ache of life, the loneliness of Death,
The insufferable sufficiency of breath.
And with Thy sword
Thou piercest very far.

Not unto us, O Lord:
Nay, Lord, but unto her be all things given.
My light, and life, and earth and sky be blasted,
But let not all that wealth of love be wasted;
Let Hell afford
The pavement of her Heaven.

HENRY CUST

A VALEDICTION FORBIDDING MOURNING

As VIRTUOUS men pass mildly away,
　And whisper to their souls to go,
Whilst some of their sad friends do say,
　"Now his breath goes," and some say, "No,"

So let us melt, and make no noise,
　No tear-floods, nor sigh-tempests move;
'Twere profanation of our joys
　To tell the laity our love.

Moving of the earth brings harms and fears;
　Men reckon what it did, and meant;
But trepidation of the spheres,
　Though greater far, is innocent.

Dull sublunary lovers' love
　—Whose soul is sense—cannot admit
Of absence, 'cause it doth remove
　The thing which elemented it.

But we by a love so far refined,
  That ourselves know not what it is,
Inter-assured of the mind,
  Care less eyes, lips and hands to miss.

Our two souls therefore, which are one,
  Though I must go, endure not yet
A breach, but an expansion,
  Like gold to airy thinness beat.

If they are two, they are two so
  As stiff twin compasses are two;
Thy soul, the fix'd foot, makes no show
  To move, but doth, if th'other do.

And though it in the centre sit,
  Yet, when the other far doth roam,
It leans, and hearkens after it,
  And grows erect, as that comes home.

Such wilt thou be to me, who must,
  Like th'other foot, obliquely run;
Thy firmness makes my circle just,
  And makes me end where I begun.

JOHN DONNE

THE RELIC

WHEN my grave is broke up again,
Some second guest to entertain,
—For graves have learn'd that woman-head,
To be to more than one a bed—
  And he that digs it, spies
A bracelet of bright hair about the bone,
  Will not he let us alone,
And think that there a loving couple lies,
Who thought that this device might be some way
To make their souls at the last busy day
Meet at this grave, and make a little stay?

If this fall in a time, or land,
Where mass-devotion doth command,
Then he that digs us up will bring
Us to the bishop or the king,
  To make us relics; then
Thou shalt be a Mary Magdalen, and I
  A something else thereby;
All women shall adore us, and some men.
And since at such times miracles are sought,
I would have that age by this paper taught
What miracles we harmless lovers wrought.

JOHN DONNE

First, we loved well and faithfully,
  Yet knew not what we loved, nor why;
Difference of sex we never knew,
No more than guardian angels do;
  Coming and going we
Perchance might kiss, but not between those meals;
  Our hands ne'er touched the seals,
Which nature, injured by late law, sets free.
These miracles we did; but now alas!
All measure, and all language, I should pass,
Should I tell what a miracle she was.

JOHN DONNE

THE PARTING

SINCE there's no help, come let us kiss and part—
Nay, I have done, you get no more of me;
And I am glad, yea, glad with all my heart,
That thus so cleanly I myself can free.
Shake hands for ever, cancel all our vows,
And when we meet at any time again,
Be it not seen in either of our brows
That we one jot of former love retain.
Now at the last gasp of Love's latest breath,
When his pulse failing, Passion speechless lies,
When Faith is kneeling by his bed of death,
And Innocence is closing up his eyes,
   —Now if thou would'st, when all have given him over,
   From death to life thou might'st him yet recover.

MICHAEL DRAYTON

THE GOING

WHY DID you give no hint that night
That quickly after the morrow's dawn,
And calmly, as if indifferent quite,
You would close your term here, up and be gone
    Where I could not follow
    With wing of swallow
To gain one glimpse of you ever anon!

    Never to bid good-bye,
    Or give me the softest call,
Or utter a wish for a word, while I
Saw morning harden upon the wall,
    Unmoved, unknowing
    That your great going
Had place *that* moment, and altered all.

Why do you make me leave the house
And think for a breath it is you I see
At the end of the alley of bending boughs
Where so often at dusk you used to be;
    Till in gathering dankness
    The yawning blackness
Of the perspective sickens me!

THOMAS HARDY

You were she who abode
By those red-veined rocks far West,
You were the swan-necked one who rode
Along the beetling Beening Crest,
    And, reining nigh me,
    Would muse and eye me,
While Life unrolled us its very best.

Why, then, latterly did we not speak,
Did we not think of those days long dead,
And ere your vanishing strive to seek
That time's renewal? We might have said,
    "In this bright weather
    We'll visit together
Those places that once we visited."

Well, well! All's past amend,
    Unchangeable. It must go.
I seem but a dead man held on end
To sink down soon...O you could not know
    That such swift fleeing
    No soul foreseeing—
Not even I—would undo me so!

                                    THOMAS HARDY

WHAT IS TO COME WE KNOW NOT

WHAT is to come we know not. But we know
That what has been was good—was good to show,
Better to hide, and best of all to bear.
We are the masters of the days that were:
We have lived, we have loved, we have suffered...
even so.

Shall we not take the ebb who had the flow?
Life was our friend. Now, if it be our foe—
Dear, though it spoil and break us!—need we care
What is to come?

Let the great winds their worst and wildest blow,
Or the gold weather round us mellow slow:
We have fulfilled ourselves, and we can dare
And we can conquer, though we may not share
In the rich quiet of the afterglow
What is to come.

WILLIAM ERNEST HENLEY

FAIN WOULD I CHANGE THAT NOTE

Fain would I change that note
    To which fond Love hath charmed me
Long, long to sing by rote,
Fancying that that harm'd me.
Yet when this thought doth come,
'Love is the perfect sum
    Of all delight,'
I have no other choice
Either for pen or voice
    To sing or write.

O love, they wrong thee much
That say thy sweet is bitter,
When thy rich fruit is such
As nothing can be sweeter.
Fair house of joy and bliss,
Where truest pleasure is,
    I do adore thee:
I know thee what thou art,
I serve thee with my heart,
    And fall before thee.

CAPTAIN TOBIAS HUME

TO CELIA

Drink to me only with thine eyes,
 And I will pledge with mine;
Or leave a kiss but in the cup
 And I'll not look for wine.
The thirst that from the soul doth rise,
 Doth ask a drink divine;
But might I of Jove's nectar sup,
 I would not change for thine.

I sent thee late a rosy wreath,
 Not so much honouring thee
As giving it a hope that there
 It could not wither'd be;
But thou thereon didst only breathe,
 And sent'st it back to me;
Since when it grows, and smells, I swear,
 Not of itself but thee!

BEN JONSON

SONNET

WRITTEN ON A BLANK PAGE IN SHAKESPEARE'S POEMS,

FACING

A LOVER'S COMPLAINT

BRIGHT STAR, would I were steadfast as thou art—
Not in lone splendour hung aloft the night,
And watching, with eternal lids apart,
Like Nature's patient sleepless Eremite,
The moving waters at their priest-like task
Of pure ablution round earth's human shores,
Or gazing on the new soft-fallen mask
Of snow upon the mountains and the moors—
No—yet still steadfast, still unchangeable,
Pillow'd upon my fair love's ripening breast,
To feel for ever its soft fall and swell,
Awake for ever in a sweet unrest,
Still, still to hear her tender-taken breath,
And so live ever—or else swoon to death.

JOHN KEATS

LA BELLE DAME SANS MERCI

O WHAT can ail thee, knight-at-arms,
    Alone and palely loitering?
The sedge is wither'd from the lake,
    And no birds sing.

O what can ail thee, knight-at-arms,
    So haggard, and so woe-begone?
The squirrel's granary is full,
    And the harvest's done.

I see a lily on thy brow,
    With anguish moist and fever dew;
And on thy cheek a fading rose
    Fast withereth too.

I met a lady in the meads
    Full beautiful, a faery's child,
Her hair was long, her foot was light,
    And her eyes were wild.

I made a garland for her head,
  And bracelets too, and fragrant zone;
She look'd at me as she did love,
  And made sweet moan.

I set her on my pacing steed,
  And nothing else saw all day long,
For sideways would she lean, and sing
  A faery's song.

She found me roots of relish sweet,
  And honey wild, and manna dew,
And sure in language strange she said,
  "I love thee true."

She took me to her elfin grot,
  And there she wept and sigh'd full sore,
And there I shut her wild, wild eyes—
  With kisses four.

And there we slumbred on the moss,
  And there I dream'd—Ah! woe betide!
The latest dream I ever dream'd
  On the cold hill side.

I saw pale kings, and princes too,
  Pale warriors, death-pale were they all;
Who cried—"La Belle Dame sans Merci
  Hath thee in thrall!"

[83]

JOHN KEATS

I saw their starv'd lips in the gloam
  With horrid warning gapèd wide,
And I awoke and found me here
  On the cold hill side.

And this is why I sojourn here
  Alone and palely loitering,
Though the sedge is wither'd from the lake,
  And no birds sing.

JOHN KEATS

AIRLY BEACON

AIRLY Beacon, Airly Beacon;
  O the pleasant sight to see
Shires and towns from Airly Beacon,
  While my love climb'd up to me!

Airly Beacon, Airly Beacon;
  O the happy hours we lay
Deep in fern on Airly Beacon,
  Courting through the summer's day!

Airly Beacon, Airly Beacon;
  Oh the weary haunt for me,
All alone on Airly Beacon,
  With his baby on my knee!

CHARLES KINGSLEY

THE LOVE SONG OF HAR DYAL

Alone upon the housetops, to the North
   I turn and watch the lightning in the sky,—
The glamour of thy footsteps in the North,
   Come back to me, Belovèd, or I die!

Below my feet the still bazar is laid,
   Far, far, below the weary camels lie,—
The camels and the captives of thy raid.
   Come back to me, Belovèd, or I die!

My father's wife is old and harsh with years,
   And drudge of all my father's house am I.—
My bread is sorrow and my drink is tears,
   Come back to me, Belovèd, or I die!

RUDYARD KIPLING

SEPARATION

THERE is a mountain and a wood between us,
Where the lone shepherd and late bird have seen us
  Morning and noon and eventide repass.
Between us now the mountain and the wood
Seem standing darker than last year they stood,
  And say we must not cross—alas! alas!

WALTER SAVAGE LANDOR

ROSE AYLMER

Ah, what avails the sceptred race,
   Ah, what the form divine!
What every virtue, every grace!
   Rose Aylmer, all were thine.

Rose Aylmer, whom these wakeful eyes
   May weep, but never see,
A night of memories and sighs
   I consecrate to thee.

                WALTER SAVAGE LANDOR

SONG

O STAY, Madonna! stay;
   'Tis not the dawn of day
That marks the skies with yonder opal streak:
   The stars in silence shine;
   Then press your lips to mine,
And rest upon my neck thy fervid cheek.

   O sleep, Madonna! sleep:
   Leave me to watch and weep
O'er the sad memory of departed joys,
   O'er hope's extinguished beam,
   O'er fancy's vanished dream,
O'er all that nature gives and man destroys.

   O wake, Madonna! wake;
   Even now the purple lake
Is dappled o'er with flakes of amber light;
   A glow is on the hill
   And every trickling rill
In golden threads leaps down from yonder height.

LORD MACAULAY

O fly, Madonna! fly,
Lest day and envy spy
What only love and night may safely know:
Fly, and tread softly, dear!
Lest those who hate us, hear
The sound of thy light footsteps as they go.

LORD MACAULAY

From "DR. FAUSTUS"

Was this the face that launch'd a thousand ships?
And burnt the topless towers of Ilium?
Sweet Helen, make me immortal with a kiss:
Her lips suck forth my soul, see where it flies;
Come Helen, come, give me my soul again,
Here will I dwell, for Heaven is in these lips,
And all is dross that is not Helena.
I will be Paris, and for love of thee,
Instead of Troy shall Wittenberg be sack'd,
And I will combat with weak Menelaus,
And wear thy colours on my plumèd crest.
Yea, I will wound Achilles in the heel,
And then return to Helen for a kiss.
O thou art fairer than the evening's air,
Clad in the beauty of a thousand stars:
Brighter art thou than flaming Jupiter,
When he appear'd to hapless Semele:
More lovely than the monarch of the sky,
In wanton Arethusa's azure arms,
And none but thou shalt be my paramour.

CHRISTOPHER MARLOWE

TO HIS COY MISTRESS

Had we but world enough, and time,
This coyness, Lady, were no crime.
We would sit down, and think which way
To walk, and pass our long love's day.
Thou by the Indian Ganges' side
Shouldst rubies find: I by the tide
Of Humber would complain. I would
Love you ten years before the Flood,
And you should, if you please, refuse
Till the conversion of the Jews.
My vegetable love should grow
Vaster than empires and more slow;
An hundred years should go to praise
Thine eyes, and on thy forehead gaze;
Two hundred to adore each breast,
But thirty thousand to the rest;
An age at least to every part,
And the last age should show your heart.
For, lady, you deserve this state,
Nor would I love at lower rate.
But at my back I always hear
Time's winged chariot hurrying near;

And yonder all before us lie
Deserts of vast eternity.
Thy beauty shall no more be found,
Nor, in thy marble vault, shall sound
My echoing song; then worms shall try
That long-preserved virginity,
And your quaint honour turn to dust,
And into ashes all my lust:
The grave's a fine and private place,
But none, I think, do there embrace.

  Now, therefore, while the youthful hue
Sits on thy skin like morning dew,
And while thy willing soul transpires
At every pore with instant fires,
Now let us sport us while we may,
And now, like amorous birds of prey,
Rather at once our time devour,
Than languish in his slow-chapt power.
Let us roll all our strength and all
Our sweetness up into one ball,
And tear our pleasures with rough strife,
Thorough the iron gates of life:
Thus, though we cannot make our sun
Stand still, yet we can make him run.

ANDREW MARVELL

From LOVE IN THE VALLEY

Hither she comes; she comes to me; she lingers,
  Deepens her brown eyebrows, while in new surprise
High rise the lashes in wonder of a stranger;
  Yet am I the light and living of her eyes.
Something friends have told her fills her heart to brimming,
  Nets her in her blushes, and wounds her, and tames.—
Sure of her haven, O like a dove alighting,
  Arms up, she dropp'd: our souls were in our names.

Soon will she lie like a white frost sunrise.
  Yellow oats and brown wheat, barley pale as rye,
Long since your sheaves have yielded to the thresher,
  Felt the girdle loosen'd, seen the tresses fly.
Soon will she lie like a blood-red sunset,
  Swift with the to-morrow, green-wing'd Spring!
Sing from the South-west, bring back her truants,
  Nightingale and swallow, song and dipping wing.

· · · ·

Could I find a place to be alone with heaven,
  I would speak my heart out: heaven is my need.
Every woodland tree is flushing like the dogwood,
  Flashing like the whitebeam, swaying like the reed.

GEORGE MEREDITH

Flushing like the dogwood crimson in October;
  Streaming like the flag-weed South-west blown;
Flashing as in gusts the sudden-lighted whitebeam
  All seem to know what is for heaven alone.

GEORGE MEREDITH

MODERN LOVE

Sonnet XLVII

We saw the swallows gathering in the sky,
And in the osier-isle we heard them noise.
We had not to look back on summer joys,
Or forward to a summer of bright dye:
But in the largeness of the evening earth
Our spirits grew as we went side by side.
The hour became her husband and my bride.
Love, that had robbed us so, thus blessed our dearth!
The pilgrims of the year waxed very loud
In multitudinous chatterings, as the flood
Full brown came from the West, and like pale blood
Expanded to the upper crimson cloud.
Love, that had robbed us of immortal things,
This little moment mercifully gave,
Where I have seen across the twilight wave
The swan sail with her young beneath her wings.

GEORGE MEREDITH

MODERN LOVE

Sonnet L

Thus piteously Love closed what he begat:
The union of this ever-diverse pair!
These two were rapid falcons in a snare,
Condemned to do the flitting of the bat.
Lovers beneath the singing sky of May,
They wandered once; clear as the dew on flowers:
But they fed not on the advancing hours;
Their hearts held cravings for the buried day.
Then each applied to each that fatal knife,
Deep questioning, which probes to endless dole.
Ah, what a dusty answer gets the soul
When hot for certainties in this our life!—
In tragic hints here see what evermore
Moves dark as yonder midnight ocean's force,
Thundering like ramping hosts of warrior horse,
To throw that faint thin line upon the shore!

GEORGE MEREDITH

RENOUNCEMENT

I MUST not think of thee; and, tired yet strong,
  I shun the love that lurks in all delight—
  The thought of thee—and in the blue heaven's height,
And in the dearest passage of a song.
Oh, just beyond the fairest thoughts that throng
  This breast, the thought of thee waits hidden yet bright;
  But it must never, never come in sight;
I must stop short of thee the whole day long.
But when Sleep comes to close each difficult day,
  When night gives pause to the long watch I keep,
And all my bonds I needs must loose apart,
Must doff my will as raiment laid away,—
  With the first dream that comes with the first sleep
I run, I run, I am gather'd to thy heart.

ALICE MEYNELL

A FAREWELL

WITH ALL my will, but much against my heart,
We two now part.
My very Dear,
Our solace is, the sad road lies so clear.
It needs no art,
With faint, averted feet,
And many a tear,
In our opposèd paths to persevere.
Go thou to East, I West.
We will not say
There's any hope, it is so far away.
But, O, my Best,
When the one darling of our widowhead,
The nursling Grief,
Is dead,
And no dews blur our eyes
To see the peach-bloom come in evening skies,
Perchance we may,
Where now this night is day,
And ever through faith of still-averted feet,
Making full circle of our banishment,
Amazèd meet;

COVENTRY PATMORE

The bitter journey to the bourne so sweet
Seasoning the termless feast of our content
With tears of recognition never dry.

COVENTRY PATMORE

TO HELEN

Helen, thy beauty is to me
Like those Nicèan barks of yore
That gently, o'er a perfumed sea,
    The weary way-worn wanderer bore
    To his own native shore.

On desperate seas long wont to roam,
    Thy hyacinth hair, thy classic face,
Thy Naiad airs have brought me home
    To the glory that was Greece,
And the grandeur that was Rome.

Lo, in yon brilliant window-niche
    How statue-like I see thee stand,
    The agate lamp within thy hand,
Ah! Psyche, from the regions which
    Are holy land!

EDGAR ALLAN POE

A BRIDE SONG

Through the vales to my love!
  To the happy small nest of home
Green from basement to roof;
  Where the honey-bees come
To the window-sill flowers,
  And dive from above,
Safe from the spider that weaves
  Her warp and her woof
In some outermost leaves.

Through the vales to my love!
  In sweet April hours
  All rainbows and showers,
While dove answers dove,—
  In beautiful May,
When the orchards are tender
  And frothing with flowers,—
  In opulent June,
When the wheat stands up slender
  By sweet-smelling hay,
And half the sun's splendour
  Descends to the moon.

CHRISTINA ROSSETTI

Through the vales to my love!
  Where the turf is so soft to the feet
  And the thyme makes it sweet,
And the stately foxglove
  Hangs silent its exquisite bells;
The greenness grows greener,
  And bulrushes stand
Round a lily to screen her.

Nevertheless, if this land,
  Like a garden to smell and to sight,
Was turned to a desert of sand;
  Stripped bare of delight,
  All its best gone to worst,
For my feet no repose,
  No water to comfort my thirst,
And heaven like a furnace above,—
  The desert would be
  As gushing of waters to me,
The wilderness be as a rose,
  If it led me to thee,
  O my love.

CHRISTINA ROSSETTI

REMEMBER

Remember me when I am gone away,
   Gone far away into the silent land;
   When you can no more hold me by the hand,
Nor I half turn to go, yet turning stay.
Remember me when no more day by day
   You tell me of our future that you plann'd:
   Only remember me; you understand
It will be late to counsel then or pray.
Yet if you should forget me for a while
   And afterwards remember, do not grieve:
   For if the darkness and corruption leave
   A vestige of the thoughts that once I had,
Better by far you should forget and smile
   Than that you should remember and be sad.

CHRISTINA ROSSETTI

SONG

When I am dead, my dearest,
  Sing no sad songs for me;
Plant thou no roses at my head,
  Nor shady cypress tree:
Be the green grass above me
  With showers and dewdrops wet;
And if thou wilt, remember,
  And if thou wilt, forget.

I shall not see the shadows,
  I shall not feel the rain;
I shall not hear the nightingale
  Sing on, as if in pain;
And dreaming through the twilight
  That doth not rise nor set,
Haply I may remember,
  And haply may forget.

CHRISTINA ROSSETTI

A BIRTHDAY

My heart is like a singing bird
  Whose nest is in a water'd shoot;
My heart is like an apple-tree
  Whose boughs are bent with thick-set fruit;
My heart is like a rainbow shell
  That paddles in a halcyon sea;
My heart is gladder than all these,
  Because my love is come to me.

Raise me a daïs of silk and down;
  Hang it with vair and purple dyes;
Carve it with doves and pomegranates,
  And peacocks with a hundred eyes;
Work it with gold and silver grapes,
  In leaves and silver fleurs-de-lys;
Because the birthday of my life
  Is come, my love is come to me.

CHRISTINA ROSSETTI

THE WOODSPURGE

THE WIND flapped loose, the wind was still,
Shaken out dead from tree and hill:
I had walked on at the wind's will,—
I sat now, for the wind was still.

Between my knees my forehead was,—
My lips, drawn in, said naught, alas!
My hair was over in the grass,
My naked ears heard the day pass.

My eyes, wide open, had the sun
Of some ten weeds to fix upon;
Among these few, out of the sun,
The woodspurge flowered, three cups in one.

From perfect grief there need not be
Wisdom or even memory:
One thing then learnt remains to me,—
The woodspurge has a cup of three.

DANTE GABRIEL ROSSETTI

SONNETS FROM THE HOUSE OF LIFE

Supreme Surrender

To all the spirits of Love that wander by
  Along his love-sown harvest-field of sleep,
  My lady lies apparent; and the deep
Calls to the deep; and no man sees but I.
The bliss so long afar, at length so nigh,
  Rests there attained. Methinks proud Love must weep
  When Fate's control doth from his harvest reap
The sacred hour for which the years did sigh.

First touched, the hand now warm around my neck
  Taught memory long to mock desire; and lo!
  Across my breast the abandoned hair doth flow,
Where one shorn tress long stirred the longing ache:
And next the heart that trembled for its sake
  Lies the queen-heart in sovereign overthrow.

DANTE GABRIEL ROSSETTI

SONNETS FROM THE HOUSE OF LIFE

LOVE-SWEETNESS

SWEET dimness of her loosened hair's downfall
  About thy face; her sweet hands round thy head
  In gracious fostering union garlanded;
Her tremulous smiles; her glances' sweet recall
Of love; her murmuring sighs memorial;
  Her mouth's culled sweetness by thy kisses shed
  On cheeks and neck and eyelids, and so led
Back to her mouth which answers there for all:—

What sweeter than these things, except the thing
  In lacking which all these would lose their sweet:—
  The confident heart's still fervour; the swift beat
And soft subsidence of the spirit's wing,
Then when it feels, in cloud-girt wayfaring,
  The breath of kindred plumes against its feet?

DANTE GABRIEL ROSSETTI

SONNETS FROM THE HOUSE OF LIFE

Secret Parting

Because our talk was of the cloud-control
  And moon-track of the journeying face of Fate,
  Her tremulous kisses faltered at love's gate
And her eyes dreamed against a distant goal:
But soon, remembering her how brief the whole
  Of joy, which its own hours annihilate,
  Her set gaze gathered, thirstier than of late,
And as she kissed, her mouth became her soul.

Thence in what ways we wandered, and how strove
  To build with fire-tried vows the piteous home
  Which memory haunts and whither sleep may roam,—
They only know for whom the roof of Love
Is the still-seated secret of the grove,
  Nor spire may rise nor bell be heard therefrom.

DANTE GABRIEL ROSSETTI

PROUD MAISIE

Proud Maisie is in the wood,
   Walking so early;
Sweet Robin sits on the bush,
   Singing so rarely.

"Tell me, thou bonny bird,
   When shall I marry me?"
—"When six braw gentlemen
   Kirkward shall carry ye."

"Who makes the bridal bed,
   Birdie, say truly?"
—"The gray-headed sexton
   That delves the grave duly.

"The glow-worm o'er grave and stone
   Shall light thee steady;
The owl from the steeple sing
   Welcome, proud lady!"

SIR WALTER SCOTT

COUNTY GUY

Ah! County Guy, the hour is nigh,
   The sun has left the lea,
The orange flower perfumes the bower,
   The breeze is on the sea.
The lark, his lay who trill'd all day,
   Sits hush'd his partner nigh;
Breeze, bird, and flower confess the hour,
   But where is County Guy?

The village maid steals through the shade,
   Her shepherd's suit to hear;
To beauty shy, by lattice high,
   Sings high-born Cavalier.
The star of love, all stars above,
   Now reigns o'er earth and sky;
And high and low the influence know—
   But where is County Guy!

SIR WALTER SCOTT

SONNET XV

When I consider everything that grows
Holds in perfection but a little moment,
That this huge stage presenteth nought but shows
Whereon the stars in secret influence comment;
When I perceive that men as plants increase,
Cheered and check'd even by the selfsame sky,
Vaunt in their youthful sap, at height decrease,
And wear their brave state out of memory;
Then the conceit of this inconstant stay
Sets you, most rich in youth, before my sight,
Where wasteful Time debateth with Decay,
To change your day of youth to sullied night;
   And, all in war with Time for love of you,
   As he takes from you, I engraft you new.

WILLIAM SHAKESPEARE

SONNET XVIII

Shall I compare thee to a summer's day?
Thou art more lovely and more temperate:
Rough winds do shake the darling buds of May,
And summer's lease hath all too short a date;
Sometime too hot the eye of heaven shines,
And often is his gold complexion dimm'd;
And every fair from fair sometime declines,
By chance or nature's changing course untrimm'd:
But thy eternal summer shall not fade
Nor lose possession of that fair thou ow'st;
Nor shall Death brag thou wander'st in his shade,
When in eternal lines to time thou grow'st:
  So long as men can breathe or eyes can see,
  So long lives this and this gives life to thee.

WILLIAM SHAKESPEARE

SONNET XXIII

As AN unperfect actor on the stage
Who with his fear is put besides his part,
Or some fierce thing replete with too much rage,
Whose strength's abundance weakens his own heart;
So I, for fear of trust, forget to say
The perfect ceremony of love's rite,
And in mine own love's strength seem to decay,
O'ercharg'd with burden of mine own love's might.
O, let my looks be then the eloquence
And dumb presagers of my speaking breast,
Who plead for love, and look for recompense
More than that tongue that more hath more express'd.
  O, learn to read what silent love hath writ:
  To hear with eyes belongs to love's fine wit.

WILLIAM SHAKESPEARE

[115]

SONNET XXIX

When, in disgrace with Fortune and men's eyes,
I all alone beweep my outcast state,
And trouble deaf heaven with my bootless cries,
And look upon myself and curse my fate,
Wishing me like to one more rich in hope,
Featur'd like him, like him with friends possess'd,
Desiring this man's art, and that man's scope,
With what I most enjoy contented least;
Yet, in these thoughts myself almost despising,
Haply I think on thee, and then my state,
Like to the lark at break of day arising
From sullen earth, sings hymns at heaven's gate;
   For thy sweet love rememb'red such wealth brings,
   That then I scorn to change my state with kings.

WILLIAM SHAKESPEARE

SONNET XXX

When to the sessions of sweet silent thought
I summon up remembrance of things past,
I sigh the lack of many a thing I sought,
And with old 'woes new wail my dear time's waste:
Then can I drown an eye, unus'd to flow,
For precious friends hid in death's dateless night,
And weep afresh love's long since cancell'd woe,
And moan the expense of many a vanish'd sight:
Then can I grieve at grievances foregone,
And heavily from woe to woe tell o'er
The sad account of fore-bemoan'd moan,
Which I new pay as if not paid before.
But if the while I think on thee, dear friend,
All losses are restor'd and sorrows end.

WILLIAM SHAKESPEARE

SONNET XXXII

IF THOU survive my well-contented day,
When that churl Death my bones with dust shall cover,
And shalt by fortune once more re-survey
These poor rude lines of thy deceasèd lover,
Compare them with the bettering of the time,
And, though they be outstripp'd by every pen,
Reserve them for my love, not for their rhyme,
Exceeded by the height of happier men.
O, then vouchsafe me but this loving thought:
"Had my friend's Muse grown with this growing age,
A dearer birth than this his love had brought,
To march in ranks of better equipage:
   But since he died, and poets better prove,
   Theirs for their style I'll read, his for his love."

WILLIAM SHAKESPEARE

SONNET L

How HEAVY do I journey on the way,
When what I seek, my weary travel's end,
Doth teach that ease and that repose to say,
"Thus far the miles are measur'd from thy friend!"
The beast that bears me, tired with my woe,
Plods dully on, to bear that weight in me,
As if by some instinct the wretch did know
His rider lov'd not speed, being made from thee.
The bloody spur cannot provoke him on
That sometimes anger thrusts into his hide;
Which heavily he answers with a groan,
More sharp to me than spurring to his side;
  For that same groan doth put this in my mind;
  My grief lies onward and my joy behind.

WILLIAM SHAKESPEARE

SONNET LIII

What is your substance, whereof you are made,
That millions of strange shadows on you tend?
Since every one hath, every one, one shade,
And you, but one, can every shadow lend.
Describe Adonis, and the counterfeit
Is poorly imitated after you;
On Helen's cheek all art of beauty set,
And you in Grecian tires are painted new:
Speak of the spring and foison of the year,
The one doth shadow of your beauty show,
The other as your bounty doth appear;
And you in every blessed shape we know.
  In all external grace you have some part,
    But you like none, none you, for constant heart.

WILLIAM SHAKESPEARE

SONNET LVII

Being your slave, what should I do but tend
Upon the hours and times of your desire?
I have no precious time at all to spend,
Nor services to do, till you require.
Nor dare I chide the world-without-end hour
Whilst I, my sovereign, watch the clock for you,
Nor think the bitterness of absence sour,
When you have bid your servant once adieu;
Nor dare I question with my jealous thought
Where you may be, or your affairs suppose,
But, like a sad slave, stay and think of nought
Save, where you are, how happy you make those.
   So true a fool is love that in your will,
   Though you do anything, he thinks no ill.

WILLIAM SHAKESPEARE

SONNET LX

Like as the waves make towards the pebbled shore,
So do our minutes hasten to their end;
Each changing place with that which goes before,
In sequent toil all forwards do contend.
Nativity, once in the main of light,
Crawls to maturity, wherewith being crown'd,
Crooked eclipses 'gainst his glory fight,
And Time that gave doth now his gift confound.
Time doth transfix the flourish set on youth
And delves the parallels in beauty's brow,
Feeds on the rarities of nature's truth,
And nothing stands but for his scythe to mow;
 And yet, to times in hope my verse shall stand,
 Praising thy worth, despite his cruel hand.

WILLIAM SHAKESPEARE

SONNET LXVI

Tir'd with all these, for restful death I cry,
As, to behold desert a beggar born,
And needy nothing trimm'd in jollity,
And purest faith unhappily forsworn,
And gilded honour shamefully misplac'd,
And maiden virtue rudely strumpeted,
And right perfection wrongfully disgrac'd,
And strength by limping sway disabled,
And art made tongue-tied by authority,
And folly, doctor-like, controlling skill,
And simple truth, miscall'd simplicity,
And captive good attending captain ill:
   Tir'd with all these, from these I would be gone,
   Save that, to die, I leave my love alone.

WILLIAM SHAKESPEARE

SONNET LXXIII

THAT TIME of year thou mayst in me behold
When yellow leaves, or none, or few, do hang
Upon those boughs which shake against the cold,
Bare ruin'd choirs, where late the sweet birds sang.
In me thou see'st the twilight of such day
As after sunset fadeth in the west,
Which by and by black night doth take away,
Death's second self, that seals up all in rest.
In me thou see'st the glowing of such fire
That on the ashes of his youth doth lie,
As the death-bed whereon it must expire,
Consum'd with that which it was nourish'd by.
   This thou perceiv'st, which makes thy love more strong,
   To love that well which thou must leave ere long.

WILLIAM SHAKESPEARE

SONNET LXXXVII

Farewell! thou art too dear for my possessing,
And like enough thou know'st thy estimate.
The charter of thy worth gives thee releasing;
My bonds in thee are all determinate.
For how do I hold thee but by thy granting?
And for that riches where is my deserving?
The cause of this fair gift in me is wanting,
And so my patent back again is swerving.
Thyself thou gav'st, thy own worth then not knowing,
Or me, to whom thou gav'st it, else mistaking;
So thy great gift, upon misprision growing,
Comes home again on better judgement making.
   Thus have I had thee, as a dream doth flatter,
   In sleep a king, but waking no such matter.

WILLIAM SHAKESPEARE

SONNET XC

THEN HATE me when thou wilt; if ever, now;
Now, while the world is bent my deeds to cross,
Join with the spite of fortune, make me bow,
And do not drop in for an after-loss:
Ah, do not, when my heart hath scap'd this sorrow,
Come in the rearward of a conquer'd woe;
Give not a windy night a rainy morrow,
To linger out a purpos'd overthrow.
If thou wilt leave me, do not leave me last,
When other petty griefs have done their spite,
But in the onset come; so shall I taste
At first the very worst of fortune's might;
   And other strains of woe, which now seem woe,
   Compar'd with loss of thee will not seem so.

WILLIAM SHAKESPEARE

SONNET CIV

To ME, fair friend, you never can be old,
For, as you were when first your eye I eyed,
Such seems your beauty still. Three winters' cold
Have from the forests shook three summers' pride,
Three beauteous springs to yellow autumn turn'd
In process of the seasons have I seen.
Three April perfumes in three hot Junes burned,
Since first I saw you fresh, which yet are green.
Ah! yet doth beauty, like a dial-hand,
Steal from his figure, and no pace perceiv'd;
So your sweet hue, which methinks still doth stand,
Hath motion, and mine eye may be deceiv'd:
  For fear of which, hear this, thou age unbred;
  Ere you were born was beauty's summer dead.

WILLIAM SHAKESPEARE

SONNET CVI

WHEN IN the chronicle of wasted time
I see descriptions of the fairest wights,
And beauty making beautiful old rhyme
In praise of ladies dead and lovely knights;
Then, in the blazon of sweet beauty's best,
Of hand, of foot, of lip, of eye, of brow,
I see their antique pen would have express'd
Even such a beauty as you master now.
So all their praises are but prophecies
Of this our time, all you prefiguring;
And, for they look'd but with divining eyes,
They had not skill enough your worth to sing:
    For we, which now behold these present days,
    Have eyes to wonder, but lack tongues to praise.

WILLIAM SHAKESPEARE

SONNET CIX

O NEVER say that I was false of heart,
Though absence seem'd my flame to qualify.
As easy might I from myself depart
As from my soul, which in thy breast doth lie.
That is my home of love: if I have rang'd,
Like him that travels, I return again,
Just to the time, not with the time exchang'd,
So that myself bring water for my stain.
Never believe, though in my nature reign'd
All frailties that besiege all kinds of blood,
That it could so preposterously be stain'd,
To leave for nothing all thy sum of good;
For nothing this wide universe I call,
Save thou, my rose; in it thou art my all.

WILLIAM SHAKESPEARE

SONNET CX

Alas, 'tis true I have gone here and there
And made myself a motley to the view,
Gored mine own thoughts, sold cheap what is most dear,
Made old offences of affections new;
Most true it is that I have look'd on truth
Askance and strangely: but, by all above,
These blenches gave my heart another youth,
And worse essays prov'd thee my best of love.
Now all is done, have what shall have no end:
Mine appetite I never more will grind
On newer proof, to try an older friend,
A god in love, to whom I am confin'd.
    Then give me welcome, next my heaven the best,
    Even to thy pure and most most loving breast.

WILLIAM SHAKESPEARE

SONNET CXVI

Let me not to the marriage of true minds
Admit impediments. Love is not love
Which alters when it alteration finds,
Or bends with the remover to remove.
O, no! it is an ever-fixed mark
That looks on tempests and is never shaken;
It is the star to every wand'ring bark,
Whose worth's unknown, although his height be taken.
Love's not Time's fool, though rosy lips and cheeks
Within his bending sickle's compass come;
Love alters not with his brief hours and weeks,
But bears it out even to the edge of doom.
   If this be error and upon me proved,
   I never writ, nor no man ever loved.

WILLIAM SHAKESPEARE

SONNET CXIX

What potions have I drunk of Siren tears,
Distill'd from limbecks foul as hell within,
Applying fears to hopes and hopes to fears,
Still losing when I saw myself to win!
What wretched errors hath my heart committed,
Whilst it hath thought itself so blessed never!
How have mine eyes out of their spheres been fitted
In the distraction of this madding fever!
O benefit of ill! now I find true
That better is by evil still made better;
And ruin'd love, when it is built anew,
Grows fairer than at first, more strong, far greater.
  So I return rebuk'd to my content,
    And gain by ills thrice more than I have spent.

WILLIAM SHAKESPEARE

SONNET CXLI

IN FAITH, I do not love thee with mine eyes,
For they in thee a thousand errors note;
But 'tis my heart that loves what they despise,
Who in despite of view is pleas'd to dote;
Nor are mine ears with thy tongue's tune delighted;
Nor tender feeling to base touches prone,
Nor taste, nor smell, desire to be invited
To any sensual feast with thee alone:
But my five wits nor my five senses can
Dissuade one foolish heart from serving thee,
Who leaves unsway'd the likeness of a man,
Thy proud heart's slave and vassal wretch to be:
  Only my plague thus far I count my gain,
  That she that makes me sin awards my pain.

WILLIAM SHAKESPEARE

TAKE, O TAKE THOSE LIPS AWAY

Take, O take those lips away,
   That so sweetly were forsworn;
And those eyes, the break of day,
   Lights that do mislead the morn;
But my kisses bring again,
         Bring again;
Seals of love, but seal'd in vain,
         Seal'd in vain.

WILLIAM SHAKESPEARE

[*Troilus*]

WE TWO, that with so many thousand sighs
Did buy each other, must poorly sell ourselves
With the rude brevity and discharge of one.
Injurious time now with a robber's haste
Crams his rich thievery up, he knows not how.
As many farewells as be stars in heaven,
With distinct breath and consign'd kisses to them,
He fumbles up into a loose adieu,
And scants us with a single famish'd kiss,
Distasted with the salt of broken tears.

WILLIAM SHAKESPEARE

From "ROMEO AND JULIET," V:iii

[*Romeo*]   O HERE
    Will I set up my everlasting rest,
    And shake the yoke of inauspicious stars
    From this world-wearied flesh. Eyes, look your last!
    Arms, take your last embrace! And, lips, O you
    The doors of breath, seal with a righteous kiss
    A dateless bargain to engrossing death!

WILLIAM SHAKESPEARE

From "ANTONY AND CLEOPATRA," I:i

[*Antony*]

LET ROME in Tiber melt, and the wide arch
Of the rang'd empire fall! Here is my space.
Kingdoms are clay; our dungy earth alike
Feeds beast as man; the nobleness of life
Is to do thus, [Embracing.] when such a mutual pair
And such a twain can do't, in which I bind,
On pain of punishment, the world to wit,
We stand up peerless.

WILLIAM SHAKESPEARE

[*Antony*]   Oh, thou day o' the world,
Chain mine arm'd neck; leap thou, attire and all,
Through proof of harness to my heart, and there
Ride on the pants triumphing!

WILLIAM SHAKESPEARE

[*Antony*]

> I am dying, Egypt, dying; only
> I here importune death a while, until
> Of many thousand kisses the poor last
> I lay upon thy lips.

WILLIAM SHAKESPEARE

THE INDIAN SERENADE

I ARISE from dreams of thee
  In the first sweet sleep of night,
When the winds are breathing low,
  And the stars are shining bright:
I arise from dreams of thee,
  And a spirit in my feet
Hath led me—who knows how?
  To thy chamber window, Sweet!

The wandering airs they faint
  On the dark, the silent stream—
And the Champak's odours fail
  Like sweet thoughts in a dream;
The nightingale's complaint,
  It dies upon her heart;—
As I must on thine,
  O belovèd as thou art!

O lift me from the grass!
  I die! I faint! I fail!
Let thy love in kisses rain
  On my lips and eyelids pale.

PERCY BYSSHE SHELLEY

My cheek is cold and white, alas!
My heart beats loud and fast;—
O press it to thine own again,
Where it will break at last!

PERCY BYSSHE SHELLEY

WITH A GUITAR, TO JANE

Ariel to Miranda:—Take
This slave of Music, for the sake
Of him who is the slave of thee,
And teach it all the harmony
In which thou canst, and only thou,
Make the delighted spirit glow,
Till joy denies itself again,
And, too intense, is turned to pain;
For by permission and command
Of thine own Prince Ferdinand,
Poor Ariel sends this silent token
Of more than ever can be spoken;
Your guardian spirit, Ariel, who,
From life to life, must still pursue
Your happiness;—for thus alone
Can Ariel ever find his own.
From Prospero's enchanted cell,
As the mighty verses tell,
To the throne of Naples, he
Lit you o'er the trackless sea,
Flitting on, your prow before,
Like a living meteor.

When you die, the silent Moon,
In her interlunar swoon,
Is not sadder in her cell
Than deserted Ariel.
When you live again on earth,
Like an unseen star of birth,
Ariel guides you o'er the sea
Of life from your nativity.
Many changes have been run,
Since Ferdinand and you begun
Your course of love, and Ariel still
Has tracked your steps, and served your will;
Now, in humbler, happier lot,
This is all remembered not;
And now, alas! the poor sprite is
Imprisoned, for some fault of his,
In a body like a grave;—
From you he only dares to crave,
For his service and his sorrow,
A smile to-day, a song to-morrow.

The artist who this idol wrought,
To echo all harmonious thought,
Felled a tree, while on the steep
The woods were in their winter sleep,
Rocked in that repose divine
On the wind-swept Apennine;
And dreaming, some of Autumn past,

And some of Spring approaching fast,
And some of April buds and showers,
And some of songs in July bowers,
And all of love; and so this tree,—
O that such our death may be!—
Died in sleep, and felt no pain,
To live in happier form again:
From which, beneath Heaven's fairest star,
The artist wrought this loved Guitar,
And taught it justly to reply,
To all who question skilfully,
In language gentle as thine own;
Whispering in enamoured tone
Sweet oracles of woods and dells,
And summer winds in sylvan cells;
For it had learnt all harmonies
Of the plains and of the skies,
Of the forests and the mountains,
And the many-voicèd fountains;
The clearest echoes of the hills,
The softest notes of falling rills,
The melodies of birds and bees,
The murmuring of summer seas,
The pattering rain, and breathing dew,
And airs of evening; and it knew
That seldom-heard mysterious sound,
Which, driven on its diurnal round,
As it floats through boundless day,

Our world enkindles on its way.—
All this it knows, but will not tell
To those who cannot question well
The Spirit that inhabits it;
It talks according to the wit
Of its companions; and no more
Is heard than has been felt before,
By those who tempt it to betray
These secrets of an elder day:
But sweetly as its answers will
Flatter hands of perfect skill,
It keeps its highest, holiest tone
For our belovèd Jane alone.

PERCY BYSSHE SHELLEY

THE OBLATION

Ask nothing more of me, sweet;
  All I can give you I give.
    Heart of my heart, were it more,
More should be laid at your feet:
  Love that should help you to live,
    Song that should spur you to soar.

All things were nothing to give
  Once to have sense of you more,
    Touch you and taste of you, sweet,
Think you and breathe you and live,
  Swept of your wings as they soar,
    Trodden by chance of your feet.

I that have love and no more
  Give you but love of you, sweet:
    He that hath more, let him give;
He that hath wings, let him soar;
  Mine is the heart at your feet
    Here, that must love you to live.

ALGERNON CHARLES SWINBURNE

EROTION

Sweet for a little even to fear, and sweet,
O love, to lay down fear at love's fair feet;
Shall not some fiery memory of his breath
Lie sweet on lips that touch the lips of death?
Yet leave me not; yet, if thou wilt, be free;
Love me no more, but love my love of thee.
Love where thou wilt, and live thy life; and I,
One thing I can, and one love cannot—die.
Pass from me; yet thine arms, thine eyes, thine hair,
Feed my desire and deaden my despair.
Yet once more ere time change us, ere my cheek
Whiten, ere hope be dumb or sorrow speak,
Yet once more ere thou hate me, one full kiss;
Keep other hours for others, save me this.
Yea, and I will not (if it please thee) weep,
Lest thou be sad; I will but sigh and sleep.
Sweet, does death hurt? thou canst not do me wrong:
I shall not lack thee, as I loved thee, long.
Hast thou not given me above all that live
Joy, and a little sorrow shall not give?
What even though fairer fingers of strange girls
Pass nestling through thy beautiful boy's curls

As mine did, or those curled lithe lips of thine
Meet theirs as these, all theirs come after mine;
And though I were not, though I be not, best,
I have loved and love thee more than all the rest.
O love, O lover, loose or hold me fast,
I had thee first whoever have thee last;
Fairer or not, what need I know, what care?
To thy fair bud my blossom once seemed fair.
Why am I fair at all before thee, why
At all desired? seeing thou art fair, not I.
I shall be glad of thee, O fairest head,
Alive, alone, without thee, with thee, dead;
I shall remember while the light lives yet,
And in the night-time I shall not forget.
Though (as thou wilt) thou leave me ere life leave,
I will not, for thy love I will not, grieve;
Not as they use who love not more than I,
Who love not as I love thee though I die;
And though thy lips, once mine, be oftener prest
To many another brow and balmier breast,
And sweeter arms, or sweeter to thy mind,
Lull thee or lure, more fond thou wilt not find.

ALGERNON CHARLES SWINBURNE

THE TRIUMPH OF TIME

Before our lives divide for ever,
  While time is with us and hands are free,
(Time, swift to fasten and swift to sever
  Hand from hand, as we stand by the sea)
I will say no word that a man might say
Whose whole life's love goes down in a day;
For this could never have been; and never,
  Though the gods and the years relent, shall be.

Is it worth a tear, is it worth an hour,
  To think of things that are well outworn?
Of fruitless husk and fugitive flower,
  The dream foregone and the deed forborne?
Though joy be done with and grief be vain,
Time shall not sever us wholly in twain;
Earth is not spoilt for a single shower;
  But the rain has ruined the ungrown corn.

It will not grow again, this fruit of my heart,
  Smitten with sunbeams, ruined with rain.
The singing seasons divide and depart,
  Winter and summer depart in twain.

It will grow not again, it is ruined at root,
The bloodlike blossom, the dull red fruit;
Though the heart yet sickens, the lips yet smart,
   With sullen savour of poisonous pain.

I have given no man of my fruit to eat;
   I trod the grapes, I have drunken the wine.
Had you eaten and drunken and found it sweet,
   This wild new growth of the corn and vine,
This wine and bread without lees or leaven,
We had grown as gods, as the gods in heaven,
Souls fair to look upon, goodly to greet,
   One splendid spirit, your soul and mine.

In the change of years, in the coil of things,
   In the clamour and rumour of life to be,
We, drinking love at the furthest springs,
   Covered with love as a covering tree,
We had grown as gods, as the gods above,
Filled from the heart to the lips with love,
Held fast in his hands, clothed warm with his wings,
   O love, my love, had you loved but me!

We had stood as the sure stars stand, and moved
   As the moon moves, loving the world; and seen
Grief collapse as a thing disproved,
   Death consume as a thing unclean.
Twain halves of a perfect heart, made fast

Soul to soul while the years fell past;
Had you loved me once, as you have not loved;
   Had the chance been with us that had not been.

I have put my days and dreams out of mind,
   Days that are over, dreams that are done.
Though we seek life through, we shall surely find
   There is none of them clear to us now, not one.
But clear are these things; the grass and the sand,
Where, sure as eyes reach, ever at hand,
With lips wide open and face burnt blind,
   The strong sea-daisies feast on the sun.

The low downs lean to the sea; the stream,
   One loose thin pulseless tremulous vein,
Rapid and vivid and dumb as a dream,
   Works downward, sick of the sun and the rain;
No wind is rough with the rank rare flowers;
The sweet sea, mother of loves and hours,
Shudders and shines as the grey winds gleam,
   Turning her smile to a fugitive pain.

Mother of loves that are swift to fade,
   Mother of mutable winds and hours,
A barren mother, a mother-maid,
   Cold and clean as her faint salt flowers.
I would we twain were even as she,
Lost in the night and the light of the sea,

Where faint sounds falter and wan beams wade,
  Break, and are broken, and shed into showers.

The loves and hours of the life of a man,
  They are swift and sad, being born of the sea.
Hours that rejoice and regret for a span,
  Born with a man's breath, mortal as he;
Loves that are lost ere they come to birth,
Weeds of the wave, without fruit upon earth.
I lose what I long for, save what I can,
  My love, my love, and no love for me!

It is not much that a man can save
  On the sands of life, in the straits of time,
Who swims in sight of the great third wave
  That never a swimmer shall cross or climb.
Some waif washed up with the strays and spars
That ebb-tide shows to the shore and the stars;
Weed from the water, grass from a grave,
  A broken blossom, a ruined rhyme.

There will no man do for your sake, I think,
  What I would have done for the least word said.
I had wrung life dry for your lips to drink,
  Broken it up for your daily bread:
Body for body and blood for blood,
As the flow of the full sea risen to flood
That yearns and trembles before it sink,
  I have given, and lain down for you, glad and dead.

Yea, hope at highest and all her fruit,
   And time at fullest and all his dower,
I had given you surely, and life to boot,
   Were we once made one for a single hour.
But now, you are twain, you are cloven apart,
Flesh of his flesh, but heart of my heart;
And deep in one is the bitter root,
   And sweet for one is the lifelong flower.

To have died if you cared I should die for you, clung
   To my life if you bade me, played my part
As it pleased you—these were the thoughts that stung,
   The dreams that smote with a keener dart
Than shafts of love or arrows of death;
These were but as fire is, dust, or breath,
Or poisonous foam on the tender tongue
   Of the little snakes that eat my heart.

I wish we were dead together to-day,
   Lost sight of, hidden away out of sight,
Clasped and clothed in the cloven clay,
   Out of the world's way, out of the light,
Out of the ages of worldly weather,
Forgotten of all men altogether,
As the world's first dead, taken wholly away,
   Made one with death, filled full of the night.

How should we slumber, how we should sleep,
   Far in the dark with the dreams and the dews!

And dreaming, grow to each other, and weep,
   Laugh low, live softly, murmur and muse;
Yea, and it may be, struck through by the dream,
Feel the dust quicken and quiver, and seem
Alive as of old to the lips, and leap
   Spirit to spirit as lovers use.

Sick dreams and sad of a dull delight;
   For what shall it profit when men are dead
To have dreamed, to have loved with the whole
      soul's might,
   To have looked for day when the day was fled?
Let come what will, there is one thing worth,
To have had fair love in the life upon earth:
To have held love safe till the day grew night,
   While skies had colour and lips were red.

Would I lose you now? would I take you then,
   If I lose you now that my heart has need?
And come what may after death to men,
   What thing worth this will the dead years breed?
Lose life, lose all; but at least I know,
A sweet life's love, having loved you so,
Had I reached you on earth, I should lose not again,
   In death nor life, nor in dream or deed.

Yea, I know this well: were you once sealed mine,
   Mine in the blood's beat, mine in the breath,

[154]

Mixed into me as honey in wine,
  Not time that sayeth and gainsayeth,
Nor all strong things had severed us then;
Not wrath of gods, nor wisdom of men,
Nor all things earthly, nor all divine,
  Nor joy nor sorrow, nor life nor death.

I had grown pure as the dawn and the dew,
  You had grown strong as the sun or the sea.
But none shall triumph a whole life through:
  For death is one and the fates are three.
At the door of life, by the gate of breath,
There are worse things waiting for men than death;
Death could not sever my soul and you,
  As these have severed your soul from me.

You have chosen and clung to the chance they sent you,
  Life sweet as perfume and pure as prayer.
But will it not one day in heaven repent you?
  Will they solace you wholly, the days that were?
Will you lift up your eyes between sadness and bliss,
Meet mine, and see where the great love is,
And tremble and turn and be changed? Content you;
  The gate is strait; I shall not be there.

But you, had you chosen, had you stretched hand,
  Had you seen good such a thing were done,

ALGERNON CHARLES SWINBURNE

I too might have stood with the souls that stand
  In the sun's sight, clothed with the light of the sun;
But who now on earth need care how I live?
Have the high gods anything left to give,
Save dust and laurels and gold and sand?
  Which gifts are goodly; but I will none.

O all fair lovers about the world,
  There is none of you, none shall comfort me.
My thoughts are as dead things, wrecked and whirled
  Round and round in a gulf of the sea;
And still, through the sound and the straining stream,
Through the coil and chafe, they gleam in a dream,
The bright fine lips so cruelly curled,
  And strange swift eyes where the soul sits free.

Free, without pity, withheld from woe,
  Ignorant; fair as the eyes are fair.
Would I have you change now, change at a blow,
  Startled and stricken, awake and aware?
Yea, if I could, would I have you see
My very love of you filling me,
And know my soul to the quick, as I know
  The likeness and look of your throat and hair?

I shall not change you. Nay, though I might,
  Would I change my sweet one with a word?
I had rather your hair should change in a night,

Clear now as the plume of a black bright bird;
Your face fail suddenly, cease, turn grey,
Die as a leaf that dies in a day.
I will keep my soul in a place out of sight,
 Far off, where the pulse of. it is not heard.

Far off it walks, in a bleak blown space,
 Full of the sound of the sorrow of years.
I have woven a veil for the weeping face,
 Whose lips have drunken the wine of tears;
I have found a way for the failing feet,
A place for slumber and sorrow to meet;
There is no rumour about the place,
 Nor light, nor any that sees or hears.

I have hidden my soul out of sight, and said
 "Let none take pity upon thee, none
Comfort thy crying: for lo, thou art dead,
 Lie still now, safe out of sight of the sun.
Have I not built thee a grave, and wrought
Thy grave-clothes on thee of grievous thought,
With soft spun verses and tears unshed,
 And sweet light visions of things undone?

"I have given thee garments and balm and myrrh,
 And gold, and beautiful burial things.
But thou, be at peace now, make no stir;
 Is not thy grave as a royal king's?

Fret not thyself though the end were sore;
Sleep, be patient, vex me no more.
Sleep; what hast thou to do with her?
   The eyes that weep, with the mouth that sings?"

Where the dead red leaves of the years lie rotten,
   The cold old crimes and the deeds thrown by,
The misconceived and the misbegotten,
   I would find a sin to do ere I die,
Sure to dissolve and destroy me all through,
That would set you higher in heaven, serve you
And leave you happy, when clean forgotten,
   As a dead man out of mind, am I.

Your lithe hands draw me, your face burns through
     me,
   I am swift to follow you, keen to see;
But love lacks might to redeem or undo me,
   As I have been, I know I shall surely be;
"What should such fellows as I do?" Nay,
My part were worse if I chose to play;
For the worst is this after all; if they knew me,
   Not a soul upon earth would pity me.

And I play not for pity of these; but you,
   If you saw with your soul what man am I,
You would praise me at least that my soul all through
   Clove to you, loathing the lives that lie;

The souls and lips that are bought and sold,
The smiles of silver and kisses of gold,
The lapdog loves that whine as they chew,
   The little lovers that curse and cry.

There are fairer women, I hear; that may be.
   But I, that I love you and find you fair,
Who are more fair in my eyes if they be,
   Do the high gods know or the great gods care?
Though the swords in my breast for one were seven,
Would the iron hollow of doubtful heaven,
That knows not itself whether nighttime or day be,
   Reverberate words and a foolish prayer?

I will go back to the great sweet mother,
   Mother and lover of men, the sea.
I will go down to her, I and none other,
   Close with her, kiss her and mix her with me;
Cling to her, strive with her, hold her fast;
O fair white mother, in days long past
Born without sister, born without brother,
   Set free my soul as thy soul is free.

O fair green-girdled mother of mine,
   Sea, that art clothed with the sun and the rain,
Thy sweet hard kisses are strong like wine,
   Thy large embraces are keen like pain.
Save me and hide me with all thy waves,

Find me one grave of thy thousand graves,
Those pure cold populous graves of thine,
　Wrought without hand in a world without stain.

I shall sleep, and move with the moving ships,
　Change as the winds change, veer in the tide;
My lips will feast on the foam of thy lips,
　I shall rise with thy rising, with thee subside;
Sleep, and not know if she be, if she were,
Filled full with life to the eyes and hair,
As a rose is fulfilled to the roseleaf tips
　With splendid summer and perfume and pride.

This woven raiment of nights and days,
　Were it once cast off and unwound from me,
Naked and glad would I walk in thy ways,
　Alive and aware of thy ways and thee;
Clear of the whole world, hidden at home,
Clothed with the green and crowned with the foam,
A pulse of the life of thy straits and bays,
　A vein in the heart of the streams of the sea.

Fair mother, fed with the lives of men,
　Thou art subtle and cruel of heart, men say
Thou hast taken, and shalt not render again;
　Thou art full of thy dead, and cold as they.
But death is the worst that comes of thee;
Thou art fed with our dead, O mother, O sea,

But when hast thou fed on our hearts? or when,
    Having given us love, hast thou taken away?

O tender-hearted, O perfect lover,
    Thy lips are bitter, and sweet thine heart,
The hopes that hurt and the dreams that hover,
    Shall they not vanish away and apart?
But thou, thou art sure, thou art older than earth;
Thou art strong for death and fruitful of birth;
Thy depths conceal and thy gulfs discover;
    From the first thou wert; in the end thou art.

And grief shall endure not for ever, I know.
    As things that are not shall these things be;
We shall live through seasons of sun and of snow,
    And none be grievous as this to me.
We shall hear, as one in a trance that hears,
The sound of time, the rhyme of the years;
Wrecked hope and passionate pain will grow
    As tender things of a spring-tide sea.

Sea-fruit that swings in the waves that hiss,
    Drowned gold and purple and royal rings.
And all time past, was it all for this?
    Times unforgotten, and treasures of things?
Swift years of liking and sweet long laughter,
That wist not well of the years thereafter
Till love woke, smitten at heart by a kiss,
    With lips that trembled and trailing wings?

ALGERNON CHARLES SWINBURNE

There lived a singer in France of old
  By the tideless dolourous midland sea.
In a land of sand and ruin and gold
  There shone one woman, and none but she.
And finding life for her love's sake fail,
Being fain to see her, he bade set sail,
Touched land, and saw her as life grew cold,
  And praised God, seeing; and so died he.

Died, praising God for his gift and grace:
  For she bowed down to him weeping, and said
"Live," and her tears were shed on his face
  Or ever the life in his face was shed.
The sharp tears fell through her hair, and stung
Once, and her close lips touched him and clung
Once, and grew one with his lips for a space;
  And so drew back, and the man was dead.

O brother, the gods were good to you.
  Sleep, and be glad while the world endures.
Be well content as the years wear through;
  Give thanks for life, and the loves and lures;
Give thanks for life, O brother, and death,
For the sweet last sound of her feet, her breath,
For gifts she gave you, gracious and few,
  Tears and kisses, that lady of yours.

Rest, and be glad of the gods; but I,
  How shall I praise them, or how take rest?

ALGERNON CHARLES SWINBURNE

There is not room under all the sky
  For me that know not of worst or best,
Dream or desire of the days before,
Sweet things or bitterness, any more.
Love will not come to me now though I die,
  As love came close to you, breast to breast.

I shall never be friends again with roses;
  I shall loathe sweet tunes, where a note grown
    strong
Relents and recoils, and climbs and closes,
  As a wave of the sea turned back by song.
There are sounds where the soul's delight takes fire,
Face to face with its own desire;
A delight that rebels, a desire that reposes;
  I shall hate sweet music my whole life long.

The pulse of war and passion of wonder,
  The heavens that murmur, the sounds that shine,
The stars that sing and the loves that thunder,
  The music burning at heart like wine,
An armed archangel whose hands raise up
All senses mixed in a spirit's cup
Till flesh and spirit are molten in sunder—
  These things are over, and no more mine.

These were a part of the playing I heard
  Once, ere my love and my heart were at strife;

ALGERNON CHARLES SWINBURNE

Love that sings and hath wings as a bird,
  Balm of the wound and heft of the knife.
Fairer than earth is the sea, and sleep
Than overwatching of eyes that weep,
Now time has done with his one sweet word,
  The wine and leaven of lovely life.

I shall go my ways, tread out my measure,
  Fill the days of my daily breath
With fugitive things not good to treasure,
  Do as the world doth, say as it saith;
But if we had loved each other—O sweet,
Had you felt, lying under the palms of your feet,
The heart of my heart, beating harder with pleasure
  To feel you tread it to dust and death—

Ah, had I not taken my life up and given
  All that life gives and the years let go,
The wine and honey, the balm and leaven,
  The dreams reared high and the hopes
    brought low?
Come life, come death, not a word be said;
Should I lose you living and vex you dead?
I never shall tell you on earth; and in heaven,
  If I cry to you then, will you hear or know?

ALGERNON CHARLES SWINBURNE

From "MAUD"

1

O that 'twere possible
After long grief and pain
To find the arms of my true love
Round me once again!

2

When I was wont to meet her
In the silent woody places
By the home that gave me birth,
We stood tranced in long embraces
Mixt with kisses sweeter, sweeter
Than anything on earth.

3

A shadow flits before me,
Not thou, but like to thee.
Ah, Christ, that it were possible
For one short hour to see
The souls we loved, that they might tell us
What and where they be!

4

It leads me forth at evening,
It lightly winds and steals
In a cold white robe before me,
When all my spirit reels
At the shouts, the leagues of lights,
And the roaring of the wheels.

5

Half the night I waste in sighs,
Half in dreams I sorrow after
The delight of early skies;
In a wakeful doze I sorrow
For the hand, the lips, the eyes,
For the meeting of the morrow,
The delight of happy laughter,
The delight of low replies.

6

'Tis a morning pure and sweet,
And a dewy splendour falls
On the little flower that clings
To the turrets and the walls;
'Tis a morning pure and sweet,
And the light and shadow fleet.

She is walking in the meadow,
And the woodland echo rings;
In a moment we shall meet;
She is singing in the meadow,
And the rivulet at her feet
Ripples on in light and shadow
To the ballad that she sings.

7

Do I hear her sing as of old,
My bird with the shining head,
My own dove with the tender eye?
But there rings on a sudden a passionate cry,
There is some one dying or dead,
And a sullen thunder is roll'd;
For a tumult shakes the city,
And I wake, my dream is fled.
In the shuddering dawn, behold,
Without knowledge, without pity,
By the curtains of my bed
That abiding phantom cold!

8

Get thee hence, nor come again,
Mix not memory with doubt.
Pass, thou deathlike type of pain,

Pass and cease to move about!
'Tis the blot upon the brain
That *will* show itself without.

9

Then I rise, the eave-drops fall,
And the yellow vapours choke
The great city sounding wide;
The day comes, a dull red ball
Wrapt in drifts of lurid smoke
On the misty river-tide.

10

Thro' the hubbub of the market
I steal, a wasted frame,
It crosses here, it crosses there,
Thro' all that crowd confused and loud,
The shadow still the same;
And on my heavy eyelids
My anguish hangs like shame.

11

Alas for her that met me,
That heard me softly call,
Came glimmering thro' the laurels

At the quiet evenfall,
In the garden by the turrets
Of the old manorial hall!

12

Would the happy spirit descend
From the realms of light and song,
In the chamber or the street,
As she looks among the blest,
Should I fear to greet my friend,
Or to say, "Forgive the wrong,"
Or to ask her, "Take me, sweet,
To the regions of thy rest"?

13

But the broad light glares and beats,
And the shadow flits and fleets,
And will not let me be;
And I loathe the squares and streets,
And the faces that one meets,
Hearts with no love for me.
Always I long to creep
Into some still cavern deep,
There to weep, and weep, and weep
My whole soul out to thee.

LORD TENNYSON

SUMMER NIGHT

From THE PRINCESS

Now sleeps the crimson petal, now the white;
Nor waves the cypress in the palace walk;
Nor winks the gold fin in the porphyry font:
The firefly wakens: waken thou with me.

Now droops the milk-white peacock like a ghost,
And like a ghost she glimmers on to me.

Now lies the Earth all Danaë to the stars,
And all thy heart lies open unto me.

Now slides the silent meteor on, and leaves
A shining furrow, as thy thought in me.

Now folds the lily all her sweetness up,
And slips into the bosom of the lake:
So fold thyself, my dearest, thou, and slip
Into my bosom and be lost in me.

LORD TENNYSON

SHE COMES NOT WHEN NOON IS
ON THE ROSES

She comes not when noon is on the roses—
  Too bright is Day.
She comes not to the soul till it reposes
  From work and play.

But when Night is on the hills, and the great Voices
  Roll in from sea,
By starlight and by candlelight and dreamlight
  She comes to me.

HERBERT TRENCH

COME, LET US MAKE LOVE DEATHLESS

Come, let us make love deathless, thou and I,
   Seeing that our footing on the Earth is brief—
Seeing that her multitudes sweep out to die
   Mocking at all that passes their belief.
For standard of our love not theirs we take;
     If we go hence to-day
Fill the high cup that is so soon to break
     With richer wine than they!

Ay, since beyond these walls no heavens there be
   Joy to revive or wasted youth repair,
I'll not bedim the lovely flame in thee
   Nor sully the sad splendour that we wear.
Great be the love, if with the lover dies
     Our greatness past recall,
And nobler for the fading of those eyes
     The world seen once for all!

HERBERT TRENCH

SONG

Go, LOVELY Rose—
Tell her that wastes her time and me,
  That now she knows,
When I resemble her to thee,
How sweet and fair she seems to be.

  Tell her that's young,
And shuns to have her graces spied,
  That hadst thou sprung
In deserts where no men abide,
Thou must have uncommended died.

  Small is the worth
Of beauty from the light retired:
  Bid her come forth,
Suffer herself to be desired,
And not blush so to be admired.

  Then die—that she
The common fate of all things rare
  May read in thee;
How small a part of time they share
That are so wondrous sweet and fair.

EDMUND WALLER

A SLUMBER DID MY SPIRIT SEAL

A slumber did my spirit seal;
  I had no human fears:
She seemed a thing that could not feel
  The touch of earthly years.

No motion has she now, no force;
  She neither hears nor sees;
Roll'd round in earth's diurnal course;
  With rocks, and stones, and trees.

WILLIAM WORDSWORTH

LUCY

THREE years she grew in sun and shower,
Then Nature said, "A lovelier flower
On earth was never sown;
This Child I to myself will take;
She shall be mine and I will make
A Lady of my own.

"Myself will to my darling be
Both law and impulse: and with me
The Girl, in rock and plain,
In earth and heaven, in glade and bower,
Shall feel an overseeing power
To kindle or restrain.

"She shall be sportive as the fawn
That wild with glee across the lawn
Or up the mountain springs;
And hers shall be the breathing balm
And hers the silence and the calm
Of mute insensate things.

"The floating clouds their state shall lend
To her; for her the willow bend;

Nor shall she fail to see
Even in the motions of the Storm
Grace that shall mould the Maiden's form
By silent sympathy.

"The stars of midnight shall be dear
To her; and she shall lean her ear
In many a secret place
Where rivulets dance their wayward round,
And beauty born of murmuring sound
Shall pass into her face.

"And vital feelings of delight
Shall rear her form to stately height,
Her virgin bosom swell;
Such thoughts to Lucy I will give
While she and I together live
Here in this happy dell."

Thus Nature spake— The work was done—
How soon my Lucy's race was run!
She died, and left to me
This heath, this calm, and quiet scene;
The memory of what has been,
And never more will be.

WILLIAM WORDSWORTH

SHE DWELT AMONG THE UNTRODDEN WAYS

SHE dwelt among the untrodden ways
    Beside the springs of Dove,
A Maid whom there were none to praise
    And very few to love:

A violet by a mossy stone
    Half hidden from the eye!
—Fair as a star, when only one
    Is shining in the sky.

She lived unknown, and few could know
    When Lucy ceased to be;
But she is in her grave, and, oh,
    The difference to me!

WILLIAM WORDSWORTH

WHEN YOU ARE OLD

When you are old and gray and full of sleep,
And nodding by the fire, take down this book,
And slowly read, and dream of the soft look
Your eyes had once, and of their shadows deep;

How many loved your moments of glad grace,
And loved your beauty with love false or true;
But one man loved the pilgrim soul in you,
And loved the sorrows of your changing face.

And bending down beside the glowing bars,
Murmur, a little sadly, how love fled
And paced upon the mountains overhead
And hid his face amid a crowd of stars.

WILLIAM BUTLER YEATS

INDEX OF FIRST LINES

INDEX OF FIRST LINES

[181]

INDEX OF FIRST LINES

(1)